Selfie Esteem

A Generation Unmoored

Identity Crisis in Our Children

(a Christian Perspective)

By Mary Blake

Selfie Esteem

Copyright © 2017

ISBN: 9781977036421

Warning and Disclaimer

Every effort has been made to make this book as accurate as possible. However, no warranty or fitness is implied. The information provided is on an "as-is" basis. The author and the publisher shall have no liability or responsibility to any person or entity with respect to any loss or damages that arise from the information in this book.

Publisher Contact

Skinny Bottle Publishing
books@skinnybottle.com

Introduction

I'm not a psychologist. I'm not a statistician, social scientist, or pediatrician. I'm not a school administrator, teacher, guidance counselor, or youth leader. We could say, were it not for the fact that my husband and I have just raised three children (the youngest of whom is now a college freshman), that I'm not any kind of expert at all. My only expertise comes from parenting and from being part of a community of parents. We could say then, that this message is brought to you by the heart and mind of a practiced mom.

But it doesn't take an expert to see that kids today are having a hard time. I saw it in my own kids; I saw it in my friends' kids; I see it in both broken and intact families. I see it in our small Christian school and in our large but highly-rated community public schools. I see it in the newspaper, on television, and on social media. I see it manifested in depression and anxiety, in alcohol and drug abuse, eating disorders, and sadly, suicides. My pediatrician husband sees it at our local children's hospital almost every day. The kids are having a hard time.

But haven't kids always had a hard time? It's just going to *be* hard, transitioning from childhood to adulthood, right? Right. It has always been hard. But it seems somehow to be harder now than when I was a kid, at least. Kids seem to be under higher levels of stress or less able to cope with stress or both; and the transitional problems seem to begin earlier — by fourth or fifth grade instead of middle school — to go deeper and to last longer.

Let's look at some statistics that clearly quantify the problem: statistics regarding depression and suicide. Suicide is the second leading cause of death for children ages 10-18 (The Jason Foundation, 2017), with 10 to 15 percent of all teens exhibiting some degree of depression at any time (TeenHelp.com,

2016). In my own county, over 6 percent of all teenagers have attempted suicide (WATE.com, Bridgette Bjorio, May 2016). In our school, with around 100 kids per grade, that would amount to about six kids per grade or 30 of our kids if we count as teenagers the eighth through twelfth grades. While the childhood and teen suicide demographic is said to weigh more heavily on the impoverished communities, it's not uncommon to see suicide clusters in affluent areas. In my own immediate community, with a reported average household income of approximately $100,000, at least four young people have taken their own lives during the past 12 months. It is unspeakably sad and profoundly disturbing. But what is it that makes the childhood and teen years so difficult? Why are so many of our kids suffering from anxiety and depression? Why do so many beautiful kids, with so much potential, consider their lives, at least at some juncture, to be hopeless, worthless, and unbearable?

Clearly, many factors are involved. Every community is a little different. Every school, every class, every family, every child … every day. But there is no argument that the statistics represent a disturbing trend. What can we do? Toward which direction do we turn? What wrongs can be righted in the environments and experiences faced by today's children? And how can we better arm them to face life's inevitable challenges? In the following pages we will look at these difficult questions from a practical, honest, rubber-meets-the-road perspective.

This writing is the culmination of my own experiences, observations, and learning as my three children and their peers advanced through their adolescent and teen years. The perspective is my own, reinforced and amended by online research and by the shared wisdom of parents, young adults, guidance counselors, a psychologist, teachers, a school board member, and church youth directors with whom I have consulted for the purpose of this writing: people who have ongoing interactions with kids. So, while the information is drawn primarily from my own experiences and observations, it is broadened by the varied experiences of others who have graciously provided their own input to the conversation.

The book is for those who are concerned about our young people both today and tomorrow (as the factors affecting this generation will, at least to some extent, face subsequent generations as well). It is my prayer that readers (hopefully to include some interested teens and young adults), will gain from this book some understanding of the challenges faced by tweens and teens and be inspired to step into the lives of young people around them — many of whom are clearly drifting through their existence unanchored.

4

Part I

A Generation Unmoored

Chapter 1

Quiet Desperation

My husband is a hospitalist: a general pediatrician. He has worked in our community's regional children's hospital for 18 years. During the course of that time, he has become keenly aware of some disturbing trends. First, there is the prevalence of physical illnesses for which the root causes are far more social (related to abuse, neglect, or parental incompetence or dysfunction) than physical. Tragically in such cases, the care given in the hospital is little more than the rhetorical Band-Aid — if the child is to be returned to the exact environment and circumstances which produced or encouraged his illness. Sometimes my husband spends hours arranging follow-up care for a child, recognizing all the while that the family is more than likely either unable or unwilling to comply with the care plan. Removal of the child from such a situation is difficult. It requires incontrovertible evidence against the family and must be weighed against the trauma associated with separation from the family, however dysfunctional.

Second, there is the great prevalence of physical symptoms that are clearly the direct result of anxiety, a diagnosis which doctors seem reluctant to make, probably because it is also one which parents are very often entirely unwilling to accept. Abdominal pain, inability to eat or retain nourishment, inability to stand, headache, and generalized pain are just a few of the symptoms for which test after test may be run at a family's insistence *even after it has become abundantly clear* (to any objective onlooker) that anxiety is at the root of the problem. The most common aggravating stresses are related to school, parenting, peers or family, some grief or trauma, or a combination. Stress illness is common in children from all economic strata. From the homeless to the very wealthy, the outworkings of stress are present and problematic. My husband tells me, and not infrequently, "Sometimes I have to be more a social worker or psychologist than a pediatrician!"

It comes as no surprise, then, to read in *Time Magazine's* Oct. 7, 2016 issue that about three million teens (7 percent) suffered a major depressive episode during the course of a year, or that about 20 percent of boys and 30 percent of girls have had an anxiety disorder. It wouldn't surprise me, either, if as the article suggests, there are many, many more affected teens whose conditions are going untreated and whose numbers are not reflected in these statistics (Susanna Schrobsdorff, *Time Magazine,* Oct. 2016). No one is happy or proud to be included among those who suffer from insecurities, let alone depression or anxiety, and least of all adolescents, who are fighting so desperately to be seen as strong, confident, independent young adults. Further, it is likely that among those children who might admit their need and be convinced to receive help, a number are deterred by their parents. Why? Because parents are often reluctant to see and acknowledge what is perceived (at least at some level) to be a flaw in their child *and therefore a mark against their own competence as parents.*

Then there are the suicides. We have already noted in our introduction that suicide is the second leading cause of death among adolescents and teens. In addition it should be of great concern to us all that the number of pediatric suicides doubled during the last decade (according to the Centers for Disease

Control) as did the number of patients admitted to children's hospitals for thoughts of suicide or self-harm (according to the American Academy of Pediatrics).

But what kind of kid commits suicide? The Jason Foundation, a parent resource program, lists some of the demographics within which suicide is more prevalent. In terms of gender there are four times as many males as females (though females make three times the attempts). Ethnically, suicide is most frequent among Native American and Native Alaskan youth; next Caucasian, and next, African American. But Hispanics more frequently report attempts than do the former two groups. LGBTQ youth (those who do not identify clearly with traditional sexual orientations) are considered to be at higher risk, although The Jason Foundation does not present statistics of suicide counts for this group.

A wide variety of risk factors are cited by the Jason Foundation, including mental illness or depression; substance abuse; violent behavior; violent, abusive, or otherwise dysfunctional home life; violent community; trouble in school (academic, social, or behavioral); cultural factors (gender confusion or unconventionality, racism, etc.); grief or trauma including divorce or death, illness or injury; social isolation; or the breakup of a dating relationship. Even a learning disability or perfectionistic personality can be a significant factor. Most alarming to engaged parents (and to our children as well, though they may not acknowledge or express it) is the fact that, at least from the outside looking in, it appears that *any* kind of kid could commit suicide.

My daughter and her class lost a classmate to suicide during their freshman year at our small Christian school. I didn't know him well, but he was seen by those who did know him as a quiet, kind boy and a good friend, smart and funny and witty, who did well in school and never caused any trouble of any kind. He came from an intact family and had a younger sibling, a few very close friends, and a close extended family. As stated in The Jason Foundation's information: (associated with the suicide demographic) "... there is really no 'stereotypical type' young person ... Suicide knows no boundaries; it occurs across all ages, economic, social, and ethnic boundaries." We can't generalize; the statistics serve only to help us recognize trends which might enable us to understand and address the problem.

The Centers for Disease Control's recommended strategies for the prevention of youth suicides include the training of educators and youth workers to recognize at-risk students; suicide education for youth (including risk factors and intervention); screenings and referrals; peer support programs; suicide crisis hotlines; restriction of highly lethal methods of suicide; and after the event of a suicide, a proactive response aimed at seeing schoolmates safely through the crisis (CDC, September 2017). Each of these measures is appropriate and necessary, but how can we achieve intervention before the crisis, before the anxiety or depression or isolation, long before the dawning of that terrible day when a young person feels as though total escape is the only answer?

Suicide is not the problem. Suicide is not even fully representative of the problem; rather it is a clearly visible and very painful evidence of the problem. It calls our attention. It makes us aware. It tells us that our kids are struggling.

Why would a kid commit suicide? For attention or revenge? On impulse? Maybe, but it is hard to imagine that a young person would end his life, even to gain attention or to exact revenge, unless he saw no point in going on —no other way to deal with the underlying problems. It is hard to imagine that such a self-destructive impulse would arise without a profound sense of hopelessness and desperation at least in that one moment —a conviction that life was unbearable, that things would never get better.

It goes without saying that some children, very sadly, are suffering through what might be objectively recognized as terrible circumstances: continuous hunger or danger or abuse, loss of family members to violence, substance addiction, and/or continuing illness. We can understand anxiety or depression related to such traumas. Such circumstances require immediate interventions that go beyond the scope of this book. The eradication of societal ills such as poverty, violence, neglect, abuse, and addiction is obviously a never-ending battle which must nevertheless be fought on every front. Death and disease, too, are constants with which we must forever contend. But it should be of great concern to each of us that even in the absence of such hardships (at least in their more observable forms), it seems there is a quiet desperation overtaking far too many of our youth. What are the causes of this, and what can we do to stem the tide of desperation?

In this book we will organize causes into four general categories that seem to come up over and over again: culture, compromised family structure, technology and social media, and the pressure to succeed. In the following chapters we will discuss each of these very important challenges and then turn our attention to another, often overlooked factor, which I believe supersedes even these four.

Chapter 2

Culture

"Culture," says *Cambridge Dictionary*, "is a people's way of life, especially as shown in our behavior and habits, attitudes toward one another, and moral and religious beliefs." Our culture largely determines the context within which our children grow up. Culture begins at home but extends outward to even the most distant influences, which in today's world are far more distant and varied than even 20 years ago. It determines the values, ideas, and priorities that are promoted around us. The primary influence on a child, of course, is the home —if there is an identifiable home with engaged adults to interact meaningfully with the child on an ongoing basis. Traditionally in the United States the church and community would have come second, but today the media, which permeates the home and every other life context, has largely usurped those roles. After the cultures of home, church, and community would have come the national, followed by foreign cultures, but these are now brought closer to home through various media.

So what is wrong with our culture that it would contribute to the quiet desperation of today's young people? I propose that there are at least seven major problems: disunity in our nation, communities, and homes; lack of a guiding faith; poverty and violence; terrorism; the happiness priority; emphasis on physical appearance along with sexualization; and entitlement.

Disunity

Disunity is nothing new. It's a condition of humanity. No two people agree on everything. They never have, and they never will. So what is it that's new?

First, there's the family disunity which results from the prevalence of divorce. Nearly half of all marriages in the U.S. now end in divorce. In addition to legal divorces, we have the many breakups (or non-relationships) of parental pairs who never married. "But these divorces or breakups actually relieve the disunity within the home," many have argued, and certainly there are situations in which that is the case. But divorce rarely ever improves the relationship between two parents, and to a child, well-managed conflict in the home is far better than the loss of the family unit. Yes, there were probably some marriages in the "old days," when divorce was taboo, that would best have been dissolved. But that was when people stayed married, no matter what, because they had made a commitment. Today we err to the opposite extreme — people on the whole seem to regard the marriage commitment very lightly. If we were not so cavalier in our attitudes toward both our marriages (from the first date until the "last straw") and our obligations to our children, I believe many more marriages could last and actually be healthy, mutually gratifying relationships. Today we are focused far too intently on our own needs and wants — to the detriment others — most notably our own children.

We have tried for years to say that divorce doesn't hurt the children. This is wishful thinking and highly convenient for parents who are or wish to be divorced. But it's also a lie. Just ask any child (who has not been coached to respond with political correctness) and he or she will tell you. Divorce does hurt the children. Yes, even when the marriage wasn't good — even when the divorce is necessary in order to protect the children; rest assured, divorce does hurt the children.

Second, there's a national/regional disunity, stemming at least in part from the great diversity of ethnicities, cultures, and ideologies pouring full force into the "melting pot" of our U.S. national culture. This disunity, while not exactly new, has in recent years become stronger and more palpable. Let me hasten to say that neither races nor ethnicities are themselves a problem —

we must reject entirely any insinuation that two peoples are inherently different in value because of their genetic makeup or heritage. The problem, rather, is the turbulence caused by the collision of opposing perspectives.

When the United States was founded on the basis of equality, grounded in that great truth that "All men are created equal ... endowed by their Creator with certain unalienable rights ... life, liberty and the pursuit of happiness;" when as a nation she welcomed people of all races, colors, and creeds; when she naturalized them and gave them the right to vote, an absolute future certainty was introduced. It was then predetermined that our nation would be comprised of a great variety of people having a great variety of ideas, and that these people all together would decide the nation's future.

The outworking of our nation's founding is evident in our composition of our country today, and the days in which the Judeo-Christian perspective brought by the pilgrims could be assumed as the common framework for life (and government) are past. Our Christian founders and founding weren't perfect, and neither they nor the growing nation faithfully and consistently applied the relevant Christian principles. But, for a time at least, the nation worked from a few commonly held, basic assumptions. There were some "givens" from which an argument could be presented and understood. No longer. In addition to ideological differences related to the origins of our citizenry, we have experiential differences that separate us. The experience of native and black Americans are two very clear examples.

While it is my understanding that few if any native Americans claimed to "own" land, they were, after all, the indigenous people. They should at the very least have been given every opportunity to participate in the new nation and assimilate in their native regions. Instead, all who survived the cruel drive were herded into the most infertile lands of all, to eke out their meager livelihoods while European settlers assumed ownership of the more fertile lands and the nation behind them. Many Native Americans find their circumstances little different to this day, and Native American youth represent one of the demographics at highest risk for suicide.

In the wake of the Civil War, most freed slaves owned little or nothing, were poorly educated compared to their white neighbors, and were not treated as equals. These were disadvantages which made their lives exceptionally difficult and gave them an experience and perspective which might be entirely different to that of the white family living a mile or less away. Again, the fallout continues for some black Americans as they live in poverty and instability without any real personal experience of the opportunities afforded others outside their ranks.

Multiply these profound differences of experience many times, by the Scotch-Irish who came during the potato famine; by Italians who fled poverty in hopes of prosperity; by Jews arriving as refugees during or after WWII; by refugees from Cuba, Vietnam, Somalia, Bhutan, Iraq or Iran: by immigrants from Mexico and Russia and China and Ukraine. Some, especially those who were better educated and knew English, blended easily into the melting pot. But others were not so soluble, and their disparate experiences gave them different perspectives on life.

Today in the United States we cannot be assured that a person or group to whom we speak is even able to hear us. The language we speak, the ground rules, the most basic assumptions about life may be absolutely unintelligible to the person in the seat, home, or neighborhood next to us. And how can we come to agreement when we don't even speak the same language? So we find that we are not only a diverse but also divergent nation, with diametrically opposed segments pulling us in various directions. Many of our kids therefore have little experience of solidarity with others but are faced, rather, with ongoing conflict at home, at school, and in their near communities. This is sure to contribute to instability — socially, emotionally, and ideologically.

Lack of a Guiding Faith

Another problem in the culture that surrounds many of our kids is the *lack of any guiding faith*.

There are many underlying causes of this scarcity of faith, including the diversity of ideologies we have already discussed. For many people the very existence of the great variety of ideologies not only calls them all into question but also creates an environment in which it can be easier not to espouse any faith at all than to deal with the disagreement of others who embrace another faith. Interfaith marriages also can play a role. When a close friend and I were teens, we were discussing the fact that her mother and father embraced two somewhat divergent religions (A and B). Curious, I asked her, "Do you feel more that you are more (an A believer) or (a B believer)?" Her response? "I think I feel like I'm less of either."

Another challenge to faith in the United States may be the American ideals of progress and prosperity themselves. A commitment to forward progress may encourage us to pull away from old ways and ideas indiscriminately, throwing out the proverbial baby with the bathwater. The academic community in particular, in its effort to distinguish itself as scientific and originally forward thinking, seems to make every effort to invalidate theistic faith, especially the once prevailing Christian faith, and to label its adherents as categorically weak, fearful, and simple-minded. The gift of prosperity, too, can undermine our faith by leading us to believe (at least until our world caves in around us) that we have no need of it, that it can add nothing to our lives. So we either avoid the hard questions of life entirely or we adopt a framework which answers those questions but then afford it no authority or priority in our lives. So when our children come to us with those same questions, we simply brush them aside or pat our children on the heads and assure them that they needn't worry about such things, which, as we all know somewhere deep in our hearts, is no answer at all.

Looking at faith from the Christian perspective, we can see too that one of the reasons for the diminishing numbers of Christian believers, sadly, is the failure of the church itself. People judge our ideologies more by the way we live than by any academic assessment of our system. When we as a church or as individual Christians speak or behave in an un-Christian manner, we corrupt the very ideas that we hold most sacred and give our faith a bad name. Let's make this more personal. We as parents may embrace faith, we may talk faith, and we may go through the motions of faith. But do we then invalidate that faith by the way that we think, speak, and act? Do we say to our children, without ever opening our mouths to speak it, "It's not really true," or, "It's only for children," or do we transmit that notorious old maxim, "Do as I say, and not as I do"?

Make no mistake. Our children study us; they see and they know. Do we:

1) Breach our professed faith by the way we live?

2) Negate our professed faith by the way we speak?
3) Use our faith only as it serves our purposes to protect our kids while they are yet young or to keep them in line?
4) Put our faith on the backburner, letting everything else take priority?

When we do these things, we place at risk the very foundations for life. Sobering, isn't it?

While the exact solution to the deficit of faith in our culture may be unclear, some of the results are quite clear. The internal compass is absent or at least out of order in much of our population, old and young alike. Without faith we are ultimately accountable only to ourselves. Popularity, prestige, pretty, and power rule the day as kids trample one another in their hurry to ascend the social ladder. The virtues of love, kindness, honesty, and compassion that are taught still to little nursery children (presumably only in order to establish peace at home and to create a society that protects them while they are very young) seem to go by the wayside at younger and younger ages. By age nine or 10 at least, those values are supplanted by competition, self promotion, and cynicism. Some kids are deterred by no standard of restraint when it comes to their verbal abuses of one another, especially in the context of social media, and *the level of cruelties they are willing to inflict on others is sometimes beyond imagination*.

In the absence of any faith — any authority, any guide or any lasting hope — we see in many a despondency, an apathy, and a deep sense of cynicism that result from the lack of any real sense of purpose or reason for being. In addition we have, as a society, observed two most alarming trends: the vulnerability of disaffected young people to recruitment by violent gangs (and even by terrorism) and a general *lack of compassion or respect for the sanctity of human life*.

The Exploitation of Tolerance

Yet another cultural factor related very closely to the lack of a guiding faith but so significant as to warrant a separate discussion, is the touchy topic of *tolerance*. Why would tolerance be a touchy topic? Shouldn't a nation that welcomes all races, colors, and creeds and asserts that all men are created equal (as well as the adherents to the religious traditions responsible for such ideals) be tolerant of all people? In a word, yes; but clearly not every behavior of every person. We do not currently tolerate murder, rape, assault, slander, or burglary, for example. These we absolutely do not tolerate — or should not — regardless of who commits them. So clearly it is not good that we should tolerate every behavior or word. Lines must be drawn somewhere, and we do not all agree on where they should be drawn. For that reason we have free speech and government by the people.

Tolerance as a concept in the United States has been marketed by certain sectors to the point of excess, however. By this I mean that tolerance, which originally meant making room for others, has somehow morphed into the expectation that we should applaud their behaviors. First, making room for others gave way to accepting their chosen behaviors. Accepting wasn't enough, however, for in the interest of tolerance it was demanded that acceptance give way to embracing. Nor did embracing satisfy but instead gave way to endorsement. Endorsement, too, failed to satisfy and has finally given way to adulation. Those who are unwilling gladly to render the adulation are labeled as intolerant or more notably, "haters," a judgement which seems (ironically), rather intolerant.

Into this category also falls the co-opted concept of "differences." During recent decades we have put great emphasis upon teaching ourselves and our children to embrace the differences of others. Skin color, weight, ethnicity, gender, age, blindness, deafness, developmental delays, and physical disabilities. And isn't this all right and good? Certainly! But over the years, the definition of "differences" has been expanded to include whatever course a person chooses to pursue. And while we do need always to embrace differences such as those in the list above, we are *not* obligated to embrace life courses, behaviors, and beliefs, and *ought not* if we believe them to be detrimental either to those practicing them or to others affected by them.

In the case of courses, behaviors, and beliefs, then, I would distinguish as follows. I should embrace the person whose course, beliefs or behavior are different from mine, but I may not also embrace his or her differences. I embrace the person who is different but *not necessarily* the "differences." By embracing the person who is different, I mean that I am kind, respectful, and compassionate toward him or her *as a person*. I recognize that he or she has value — that his or her life matters — as we have grown accustomed to say. And his or her life *does* matter!

So I embrace the person whose behavior seems wrong or unhealthy to me, but I am in *no way* obligated to embrace his behavior. I might in fact have to set a boundary to protect myself or others from him or her or even to report the activity to an authority. I embrace the drug addict as best I can given the problems introduced by the addiction, but I do not embrace the drug habit. I embrace the negligent serial parent who hops from relationship to relationship and does not provide proper care for the children as best I can given the problems introduced by the behavior (my first concern will rightly be for the children) but I do not embrace the dereliction.

As the result of the new "tolerance," many unhealthy behaviors and most particularly those related to sexual gratification (an assumed "right" of every individual) are justified or at the very least excused. Right and wrong are obscured, because "everything is relative." What is right for you may not be right for me, and what is right for me may not be right for you. (Note that the application of such thinking is a fallacy routinely discarded in the very moment an individual perceives that his own "rights" are compromised by the "rights" of another.)

Obviously there exists a culture of confusion when it comes to some very basic areas of life. This creates problems for young people who are trying their best to figure it all out, because any given option is said at least somewhere, by someone, to be as good as any other.

I want to reiterate, because this is such a touchy and misunderstood topic. Tolerance, making room for others regardless of their differences, is a good thing. As I expressed this idea to a friend, I accidentally typed "god thing," and it is a "God thing." We are to tolerate and affirm other people. Period. But not necessarily their ideas or behaviors. It is very clear that our nation does not tolerate every behavior (this is why we have laws and prisons), and it's also clear that we are not required as individuals to smile upon every legal behavior. Which behaviors are acceptable (and healthy) has always been a topic of debate and on the finer points, has fluctuated over time. The recent trend, however, has led us to the place where it is demanded that nearly every "alternative" idea or behavior be not only tolerated but praised. We must praise whatever course a person should choose to follow. It's the new religion. Meanwhile most every shred of traditional Judeo-Christian thinking is disrespected in many sectors.

In the current climate you're nothing (especially with respect to the popular media) if you don't embrace "alternative" behaviors as perfectly valid. So for any behavior that tempts a kid, regardless of how self-destructive, he or she can find support and supporters, at least online. Everything is acceptable, and anyone who does not accept is an idiot, and worse, a *hater*. Life is game with no boundaries and no rules; our young people are floating about in a sea of relativism, rising and falling with the tide. It's a dark and dangerous place to be.

Violence and Poverty

Violence and poverty are two cultural factors which have unquestionably negative effects on our young people. While poverty seems rarely to be cited as a factor for suicide among youths, it is related to other high-ranking risk factors such as hopelessness and depression. This comes as no surprise, since it is hard to imagine that real hunger and need wouldn't have a negative effect on the emotional health of children, whether the entire community suffers or whether a student is disadvantaged in comparison to his or her peers. But violence is a decided factor. Abuse, mistreatment, and aggression are all contributors to suicide (Stephanie S. Gardner, MD, Jan. 2017), as is the presence of a firearm in the home (Karin Kiewra, 2008).

Some communities have long been fraught with joblessness, poverty, drugs, violence, and neglect and find themselves at the center of an ongoing political debate with no real, long-term solutions in sight. But, even for kids who are not themselves exposed regularly to violence, the widely publicized events of terrorism and mass shootings (which have become far too everyday) create or contribute to feelings of insecurity, anxiety, and hopelessness among our youth. There are unanswered questions as well about our kids' saturation with violence via the programming they watch and video games they play. Discussion about the effects of such exposures is ongoing, but we know already that prolonged or frequent exposures to violent images can be detrimental to the development of young children. It seems unlikely that there is not some limit as well to the amount of exposure to violent games or programming (and the degree, nature and presentation of that violence) that would be healthy for tweens, teens, and even adults.

Happiness Priority

At an opposite extreme from the violence, need, and neglect plaguing many children in low-income and undereducated socioeconomic areas is the excessive commitment to their children's happiness endemic to many parents among the educated upper classes. Having given birth to fewer children than earlier generations and in many cases having greater ability to provide for them, it is a terrible temptation for many parents to go to any extreme to insure their children's comfort and happiness.

While it is the parents' responsibility to advocate for their children, we should *not* be their groupies, forever following them around, catering to their every whim, lauding their every breath, and defending them even when they may be in the wrong. It has been the temptation of modern-day parents to do whatever it takes to keep our children happy at all times, in every circumstance. But a child who has been appeased at every turn does not a healthy, happy adult make. After all, who will be there, when he is grown, to serve his every need?

Another strong criticism made today's parents is that we do not give children the freedom to fail. As a parent myself (and one who read and considered this criticism during my kids' elementary years), I know the pain of watching your child fail, and I understand the struggle. It's a delicate balance, and I'm sure that in some instances I missed it. But it is true that childhood failures, losses, and disappointments are a necessary training ground for our kids, providing valuable opportunities for them to learn to handle adversity.

As our parents gave us far more things and opportunities than they themselves enjoyed growing up, and as we suffered fewer hardships than they, we in the middle and upper classes have given our children far more than we had and made every effort to protect them from hardships. It's not that our kids aren't subject to stresses; they are. It's not that they don't suffer adversity; they do. But in many cases these trials are personal in nature. In other words, often it is only their own academic, social, or athletic lives (combined with their perceptions about expectations of them) that produce the stresses or adversities. They are not expected to bear much responsibility at home or to see regularly to the needs of others. They are served far more often than they serve (and their occasional service tends to receive far too much recognition and adulation). In such a context their perspectives can become very myopic, and when they don't meet their own expectations or those they believe that others hold for them, it can seem as though their whole world is crumbling.

I have observed very often that *the biggest crisis a person faces at a given time, even if very small, can feel like a major crisis*. I believe that this is far more true of my own and the following generations than of the generations before me, especially among those of us who were privileged to grow up without any major life losses. I have often said that I have led a charmed life, and in a sense this is true. As a young person I did not suffer any major personal losses, nor was it necessary for me to bear heavy responsibilities. This was indeed a great blessing; but I'm not so sure that my growing-up experience prepared and strengthened me as the real and practical hardships met by my parents during their growing-up years prepared and strengthened them.

Entitlement

Entitlement is another widely recognized problem, one that young people hate to hear about. It is true that many among the Y and Z generations exhibit the symptoms of entitlement, but in their defense, this is not entirely of their own making. The causes are varied. Some kids are accustomed, as we mentioned above, not only to having all of their needs met but to being given most of their wants as well. Whatever it is, if they want it, parents or grandparents are right there to procure it for them.

But a similar sense of entitlement also exists among children who don't have everything. Some blame this on the welfare state, which may be a contributing factor, but I believe that entitlement as an attitude has been promoted throughout every corner of American culture by means of politics, media, and advertising. As a culture we have begun to talk about rights in a way that is more comprehensive than anyone ought to expect. Where rights, life, liberty, and the pursuit of happiness, for example, were once understood as opportunities which must not be withheld from us, we now tend to see rights as products and services which should be delivered to us: the newest smartphone or laptop, maybe, designer shoes or clothing, a car, a nice apartment, a luxury vacation, an expensive college education, and on it goes. This is partly due to bids of politicians or political parties for the votes of their constituents, but it is promoted as well by the media and advertising whose primary goal is to make us discontented with what we have.

You may be able to remember a very effective advertising slogan that first aired in the 1970s when I was a kid. "*You deserve a break today,*" the jingle told us, "*so get up and get away ... to McDonald's.*" It was innocent enough; I loved that first ad as well as many of the follow-up ads using the same slogan. But perhaps there was something sinister there, something insidious, some dark shadow of trouble creeping into River City. How did McDonald's know whether I deserved a break? Perhaps I had been lazy and delinquent and deserved not a break but a kick in the pants! And yet it was advantageous for McDonald's to have me convinced that I *deserved* a break — a McDonald's break — to be specific. And I really wanted to believe. Ads tell us, sometimes very explicitly, that what we have is not enough, that we really ought to have more, better, that we *deserve* more and better. And most often the things that we are told we deserve are wants, not needs. Frequently they are luxuries.

So we are no longer satisfied with the right to the pursuit of happiness; we believe that we have the right to happiness itself. And, if we have that right, then happiness is owed to us. So whatever it is that makes us happy, if we have it we need not be thankful for it (it was an obligation, after all); and if we don't have it we are disaffected because someone, somewhere, has withheld what we are rightfully owed. This is the very definition of entitlement.

Whether because of a skewed perspective on rights (the belief that what we want, we are owed), the overindulgent parenting common in some sectors, or both, many of our kids display a sense of entitlement. And what are we teaching, if not entitlement, by assuming when our child has a problem with others (whether peers or authorities) that he is always in the right? By lauding our child for every little thing she does? By blaming others for his failures rather than helping him face and walk through them? By failing to provide appropriate consequences when she acts out? By providing his wants and never requiring him to contribute to his own or to family's needs? By giving them every right and no responsibilities? When we do these things we are training them in entitlement whether we intend it or not.

Physical Appearance and Sexualization

The last of the seven factors to be mentioned under the category of culture encompasses both our culture's *excessive emphasis on physical appearance and its sexualization of our children from an early age*. This factor requires little elaboration, because we all see very clearly in every form of media the emphasis upon sexuality and physical beauty. In a way it's nothing new; the human eye is created to appreciate beauty, and every culture seems to have had its physical idols. We enjoy looking upon beauty, whether masculine or feminine, whether child or adult, and that is why "talent" agencies are forever in search of the most attractive specimens. But, for the adolescent or teen who is becoming an adult, comparing him or herself to the models that grace the television or movie screen (and even the advertisements), each of whom seem to be so exquisitely formed, can be devastating.

It's not enough that he or she has to deal with not growing soon enough or not growing tall enough or being too round or gangling or having "weird" hair or acne or too-dark skin or too-white skin or big feet or a funny nose. On every movie, in every TV show, and in every ad, we see people with perfect hair, perfect skin, perfect teeth, perfectly-shaped noses, beautiful facial features, and exceptionally well-proportioned bodies. Yes, thankfully we do now see different colors, heights, and ethnicities in programming, but, when it comes to the protagonists, everyone is beautiful (at least after the dental work, surgery and makeup job). And frankly, in the real world we just aren't all that beautiful. So how does it make me feel, as a 10-to-18-year-old girl, when all the ads and programs feature the shapeliest women and girls with beautiful skin, hair, and features, and one look in the mirror tells me I don't have any of that? Not good, I can tell you! And that girl in the footage who's laughed at or at least pitied? She looks a whole lot more like me.

Add to that the sexualization of kids, girls especially, on screen from a very young age, even on the kids' channels. I was watching a public relations piece (ad) on an adolescent star recently, admiring her beauty and her fresh, kid-next-door appearance, when at the end of the ad she turned herself upside down in her chair, stretching her head down toward the floor, hair streaming down and legs upon the back of the chair in a most alluring pose. There was nothing indecent about it, but I wouldn't have wanted it for my daughter. The producers certainly would not have presented a boy in the same way. Nevertheless, sexual ideals are promoted in every corner, now even to the senior citizen viewership, in advertisements that imply that if you are 70 and your sex life is not what it was at 20 (when presumably it was out of this world), your life might as well be over. The messages are clear; sex is the apex of life, and you must be beautiful in order to be wanted. It's not a healthy message to anyone, let alone the young teen who has been viewing such messages for as long as he or she can remember.

Now for a public service message. Parents: You need to know that by about 10 or 11, if not before, your kids are searching for their gender/ sexual identities, most likely online, because they certainly don't want to ask you about it! The hall talk at school is riddled with sexual information, disinformation, and accusations. Your kids are informed very early that when you said "boy" or "girl," you left out a lot of information. "What am I?" they wonder. "Which one of the 37 or 51 (or whatever the current number) gender identities applies to me? And there will be plenty of information to confirm, encourage, exploit, confuse, or worry them quite thoroughly. If internet and social media are not the gender education you want for your child, you will have to be there, early and often, to provide it yourself.

Our policy as parents was to provide any and all (age appropriate) information whenever asked. In addition, we had intentional and more thoroughly informative sessions with our kids (Dad with sons and Mom with daughter) individually during preadolescence, the purpose of which was to complete their basic education and open the lines of communication. After this I felt fairly comfortable talking to my kids about topics surrounding sexuality whenever they broached the subject — or whenever something came up that I felt needed discussion. This was more information than either my husband or I received growing up, and yet I regret to inform the reader that the described education was considered by the recipients to be woefully lacking in content for their times and context. They didn't know *"anything,"* I have been told. Apparently we should have briefed them on *"everything,"* beginning with the vocabulary, either authorized or unauthorized, necessary to understand middle and high school hall talk.

In retrospect perhaps in addition to answering their questions, we should have been more proactive about addressing (within reason) any sexual content to which our kids and their peers were likely to be exposed. In this way we could perhaps have kept them better informed and created a more comfortable, day-to-day conversation.

Then there's the never-ending scourge of *pornography*. As TL Holt, a counselor in our area who regularly works with teens, so clearly stated, "Accessibility to pornographic material will continue to have a devastating impact ... increased accessibility via the internet has provided an immediate injection of objectification that can begin at any age. We see it everyday — kids playing on their parent's phones and iPads — it is only a matter of time before they unknowingly stumble upon something that can change their view of others completely."

The problem of pornography is so widely recognized and, on the other hand, tolerance of the material so implicit that I hardly know what encouragement I can give on the subject. It is very accurately a scourge, and one which due to its availability, quite literally, at our fingertips, is probably almost a rite of passage for the average teen. This is a sad reality, since exposures to pornography have an irrevocable impact. As parents we need first and foremost to keep ourselves away from it. Then we need to do all we can to educate our media-saturated children and protect them from pornography and its effects.

People, especially "old" people like me, are always complaining about modern culture, apparently oblivious to the fact that every era, their own included, has (had) both its positive and negative aspects. We must be careful about this; after all, wise King Solomon warns us never to say, "Why were the former days better than these?" For, he assures us, "It is not from wisdom that we ask this." (Ecclesiastes 7:10)

In writing this chapter I was aware that I might legitimately be accused of beating that same, old, irrelevant drum. Nevertheless. real and present cultural ills pollute the environment in which our children are growing up, and these are extremely detrimental to their health and development. It can only help to be aware of these things so that we can do our part to change them or at the very least to help our children negotiate their treacherous cultural context.

Chapter 3

Family Dysfunction, Disruption, and Dilution

The point is not even reasonably arguable: the nuclear family is to be the foundation from which our children operate as well as their first line of defense against the hostilities of the world. It is to be their source of love and security and encouragement; it is to be their safe space.

Too many kids today have no foundation to support them because the family structure is compromised or practically non-existent. We are all aware of the frequency of abandonment or removal of children to their grandparents or even a to single or widowed grandmother. Many such grandmothers are to be revered and lauded, for they are the backbones of their families, loving and serving them as the single source of stability and reliability.

All too often, however, a child is stuck in a dysfunctional home. Perhaps he loves his parent(s) — and at least at some level they probably love him — but they are incapable of providing adequate care. Too often it is the child, in fact, who has to provide emotional care for the family. He or she is left carrying burdens that he can't, that she shouldn't. This ongoing burden can be a cause for well-grounded grief and hopelessness, and it drives many children to anxiety, depression, and physical illness.

Sometimes a family is disrupted by tragedy. In such a case relatives and close friends will often circle the wagons. Tragedy seems to make strong families stronger. My mother lost her father to tuberculosis when she was four years old and her younger brother was two months old. There were five children in the family. It was a hard life, both practically and economically, but she doesn't remember it that way. She remembers having what she needed, including the love of a family who stuck together and have remained very close to this day. They understood the loss of their father, and they understood their mother's situation. They all pulled together; they all pitched in.

But the situation today is often different. As we have noted, around 50 percent of all marriages today end in divorce, with the average length of a marriage at approximately seven years. Consequently only about 46 percent of all teens aged 15-17 live with both biological parents. For black teens aged 15-17 the percentage is much lower; only 17 percent live with both parents (Paul Bedard, Feb. 2015). And the cause of divorce (or division where there has been no marriage) in most cases is not a tragedy, at least in the usual sense of the word. It is either the lack or breach of a commitment to each other and therefore *in a very real sense* to the child as well.

Of those children who live with only one biological parent, many are subject to the serial partnerships of that parent, which may be further complicated by the presence of the partners' children. 50 percent of children under the age of 13 are currently living with one biological parent and that parent's current partner (Paul Bedard, Feb. 2015).

While there are those cases in which a divorce is the only option, division of the biological parents is a tremendous loss to a child. As a culture steeped in the feminist movement, we spent years in the 70s and 80s trying to say that divorce wouldn't hurt the children ... in fact, if their parents "weren't happy together" it would be better for the children that they live separately. As we said in Chapter 2, this is absolute nonsense. Divorce always hurts the children.

I remember asking a single coworker before Christmas one year (when both he and I were young adults just out of college) what he would be doing for the holiday. I had assumed he might return home, as were most of the recent graduates in our company, since he was living and working many miles away from the state in which he grew up. Our conversation went something like this.

Me, expectantly: "What are you doing for Christmas?"

Austin: "Oh, I'm not really doing much; I'll probably just stay around here."

Me, not really sure quite what to say: "Oh. You won't go home?"

Austin: "No, I don't really have a home. My parents are divorced. If I go to my dad's, that's not home, and if I go to my mom's, that's not home, either. So probably I'll just stay here."

It is my own unproven (but completely common-sense) theory that children can understand an unavoidable hardship such as my mother's loss of her father and the necessity of all the family contributing to the family finances, or maybe a mother's divorce from an abusive father. With adequate support they will be able to bear (and even thrive under) such circumstances. But, when they cannot understand a reason for it or they perceive that the reason involves disregard for them and for their needs, the wound is deep and lasting. One that may persist into adulthood. One that they may, in fact, never quite overcome.

The truth — and it is one that gets back to our culture — is that we as a nation have become so obsessed with our own right to happiness that we cannot fully commit ourselves to the needs of our children. There is fairly wide acceptance of the philosophy that as long as one is monogamous during the term of a relationship, it is fine to move from relationship to relationship at will.

Parental divisions often result from the following:

- The couple produced a child or children with no formal commitment to one another
- The couple married for superficial reasons insufficient to sustain a marriage
- One parent wearies of his or her responsibilities or partner and pulls out, seeking "greener" pastures (which inevitably carry their own set

of problems and very often involve another less-than-perfect partner, new responsibilities, and possibly even greater difficulties).

To parental division we can add as a detriment to family stability the dilution of a child's relationships with extended family through relocation and/or the acquisition of stepfamilies. While new step-relatives may prove to be very supportive, they may also (innocently) serve to reduce the amount of time a child is able to spend with each individual grandparent, uncle, aunt or cousin in order to forge close relationships. With just one remarriage of each biological parent, a child will acquire four new "grandparents" (assuming all are living), and, if both stepparents' parents were divorced, there may be as many as eight. (Of course if we imagine that the biological parents' parents were also divorced and remarried, the child already has eight grandparents before his or her own parents' divorce.) Time with the extended family, then, becomes further and further subdivided. Add to this the geographical separations between family due to relocations and time with important grandparents, aunts, and uncles, and cousins may be very minimal.

Note that this discussion has omitted completely the stresses a child may suffer as the result of conflicts arising from the complexities inherent in blended families, including differing allegiances within the family, not to mention the more disturbing possibility of a wicked stepparent or abusive live-in boyfriend or girlfriend. (The statistics on boyfriend-related abuse are particularly disturbing).

Clearly we need to make every effort to provide the most stable possible family environment for our children, and in order to do so we must take our commitments very seriously from beginning to end. The production of children outside of marriage must not be encouraged, supported, or laughed away. Is there any hope of redemption under such circumstances? Certainly. But the goal is to provide a solid foundation for every child from start to finish.

Chapter 4

Technology and Social Media

In preparing to write this book, I posed the same question to each of those I interviewed: "What do you see as the biggest problems faced by children of ages 10-18 today?" The immediate answer, almost without fail and coming from both mature and very young adults, was related to social media, internet, or "the phone" (smartphone). While we want to be careful about using technology and "the media" as a scapegoat for every societal ill, the recent rapid advancement of technology has posed significant challenges to parents when it comes to raising our kids.

There is a lot of buzz in the media about the effects of technology and social media on our kids, and for good reason. The last 10 years have seen radical changes in kids' social behaviors and use of free time, particularly among those who have had the smartphone since their early adolescent years — we might call them the Selfie Generation.

Effect of Technology on Brain Development

Concerns about technology are not limited to the effects of internet and social media on our tweens and teens. There are valid concerns as well about the effects of technology on even the very youngest of our children. Children are introduced to devices just as soon as they can look at a screen or hold a cell phone. I have seen more than a few restaurant meltdowns either created by the removal of a parent's cell phone from a child or averted by its production for his entertainment.

Even young children are barraged on all sides by every kind of stimulus: TV, movies, computers, cell phones, video gaming devices, and — more and more — consolidated in the cell phone and laptop or tablet. A craving for the mental stimulation and instant gratification provided by interactive entertainments is cultivated at an early age. Many are worried about the effect of near-constant entertainment and information stimulus on brain development, and concerned that technology may be behind the short attention spans we see in so many of our children: their inability to delay gratification, to persevere, and to wait.

More time with devices generally means less time in physical activity, socialization, and creative play. This represents another well-founded concern about the effects of technology on children's development and overall health.

Accessible Content

The next obvious concern is the quality and nature of content to which our children have access. The opportunities for learning are beyond imagination; on the other hand our information network is infected with every corruption known to man, some of it aggressively targeting even the disinterested user. So we must be very careful — very specific — about how we search. And even then we may come across something intended to draw us off track and into the underworld. Available games and entertainment are just as diverse and carry similar risks in terms of content.

Add to this the natural curiosity of *every single healthy, growing adolescent.* They are curious about everything, and ieven if they haven't become curious, a peer, application, or the internet will present questions or information that will generate that curiosity. In 2014, in recognition of gender diversity, Facebook provided approximately 50 alternative gender options (71 in the UK), and in 2015 decided to allow custom gender identification, in case their extended list of gender options was not adequate. The latter move seems reasonable enough given the current state of affairs but the former lent credibility to all manner of unnecessary classifications, leading young tweens and teens to wonder, "If there are so many genders, which one am I?" And there is of course no end to the many entities — political, ideological, financial, predatory, etc. — who are delighted to give your child all the information they would like to have and more. Some parents just don't have time for it. Others take a very casual, liberal approach, attempting to balance any negative information with open conversation at home. And still others develop a strategy of parental controls to protect their children.

Parental controls are all well and good, necessary in fact, if your child has access to smart devices. But your child will see many things beyond the content allowed by those controls. She will look at other children's computers when they are entertaining themselves (together or working on a project) or because another child says, "Hey, look at this!" Other kids will send him materials by phone. Many schools require that your child own a device and use it at school, and the kid next to yours may not be affected by parental controls. Your child will access unprotected or public wireless networks. There are many ways around the parental controls, some of them intentional, some unintentional. There is no absolute safeguard.

Right in their own bedrooms or cars or classroom at school children can escape their upbringing and the encouragements, protections, and trainings their parents are trying to instill. They can talk to anyone, anywhere or look at anything. They get a sampling of everything, including every opinion of them and all that they have been taught to believe.

Shift from Reality to Virtuality

Another concern related to the effects of technology on our young people is the change in the way that they spend their time. Some of the restaurant meltdowns to which I referred earlier have resulted from battles between siblings over their parents' cell phones. Too often children would rather be on the phone or gaming device or watching a movie than playing outside, visiting with family or friends, or doing something creative. Years ago when my kids came along there was a popular *Sesame Street* song called, "Put Down the Duckie." The accompanying video showed Ernie struggling to play the saxophone because he didn't want to release his hold on his beloved duck toy. A far more appropriate song for today would be, "Put Down the Celly," and such advice is often just as relevant to parents as to their children.

Given the opportunity, some kids would spend almost every waking moment interacting with a device. They prefer the fantasy or virtual world to the real world. It's exciting! You don't have to wait (even for your turn), and you can shut out any unpleasant realities of life. Even your communications with other, real people can be reduced through messaging so as to eliminate face-to-face or even voice-to-voice interaction. It isn't necessary to converse spontaneously or respond in real time. If you're so inclined you can carefully control all of your interactions.

Many kids would rather isolate themselves in their rooms with their gaming than interact with others at all. And again, if they are in their rooms with their devices, they are not outdoors running and playing. Are they losing their balance in life, some wonder? Are they losing their ability to separate reality from fantasy? Are they losing their social abilities, their capacity for real conversation and honest, face-to-face communication? Are they becoming detached and developing an artificial view of humanity? Sometimes it certainly would seem so.

Messaging and Social Media

So far we have discussed three technology related concerns: possible changes in brain development, access (often unmonitored) to every form of content, and the change in the way young people spend their time. But the one that outweighs them all is the emotional impact of social media.

The challenges posed by the popularity of social media are many. We've all heard the terrible stories of sexting, sexual predators, and *cyberbullying*. We've all seen indiscretions of every kind committed on the social media outlets of the day: overly personal revelations; overly judgmental, controversial, or confrontational commentary; crude, rude, and socially unacceptable statements about others (unfortunately from adults as often as from young people). But the very young can do themselves great damage by being too raw, too honest, too emotional, by putting way too much on the line.

It is not always a child's own social media behavior that is the problem, however. Often it is the responses — or attacks — of others. Facebook, Instagram, Tumblr, and other social media sites mean a lot of things to a lot of people, but for most young people they serve primarily as outlets for personal advertisement or as experimental laboratories for identity testing. Negative responses to these advertisements or identities can, at least in the short term, be devastating.

People will say anything online — things that they would never say to anyone face to face. Kids can be very cruel in their comments. Some kids are immature and may not be able to appreciate how profoundly their comments affect others. (Look at the kinds of things people say to one another on television, after all, and we all just watch and laugh!) Other kids just don't care, because they are too busy jockeying for position within their peer group. Their philosophy much more closely resembles "survival of the fittest" than "All for one and one for all!" Depending upon the platform and how an account is set up, the negative comments of others may be displayed for all the world to see. Even if there are some privacy measures in place, no kid wants even his online "friends" to see posts or comments whose purpose is to hurt or ridicule him.

On a smaller scale we have messaging apps like Groupme and Snapchat, the primary means of communication for many kid-groups, which can be just as damaging since, again, messages may be seen by the whole group. If someone makes a tacky comment, everyone in the group knows it. Even a text or simple snapchat message can be enough to swing a teen's mood immediately from one extreme to the other.

The "Selfie Generation" are deeply concerned about how they are perceived and about their presentation of themselves on social media, especially girls. But some boys as well will spend hours working to get the best possible profile picture to present the desired image. They feel pressure to look good online, and they constantly compare themselves to others, all of whom are presenting idealized images of themselves and their "wonderful" lives. Costuming, makeup, stunts, and even social activities are conceived for the express purpose of producing a high-attention (hopefully high-status) picture or video. And kids are watching vigilantly to see how others respond. Some seem to be dependent upon near-constant feedback, regularly posting the kinds of things which encourage, beg, or even demand responses from their viewers.

A kid's whole self esteem may be tied to how others are responding to her posts or comments on social media. When someone makes a snide comment, it feels like an attack on all that she is or ever could hope to be. Add to that the fact that even happy posts, those showing friends out together having a good time (which kids post at every opportunity in part as evidence of their "awesome" social lives), are not at all happy to the kid at home on social media who is rarely or never invited to participate in any real-life social activities. It just isolates him further. It seems strange that *social media*, a resource intended to foster connection (and — *I know* — the dissemination of advertisement) should so often be mentioned in connection with *isolation*. But it's true ... while social media has great power to connect, it can also be used to isolate, and isolation may be felt even when there is no intentional effort to isolate.

Every feeling is intensified during the adolescent and teen years. Adolescents can vacillate very quickly from elation to despair, and our immediate circumstances tend to drive our feelings about ourselves during these years. Today, with the loss of privacy that comes with our kids' (voluntary or involuntary) participation in social media, their downs can be much deeper. Be it rejection, ridicule and humiliation, rash statements, indiscretions, whatever ... the information is instantly disseminated to all. The social media "like" or "dislike" drives the spirit up or down at will, jerking kids around emotionally. And they are, unwittingly, willing participants, checking their devices at every opportunity for the latest updates.

Even as adults most of us have experienced some kind of Pavlovian response to our telephones. For me it was the excitement generated by the sound of the first inquiry notifications after I began my freelance writing. Or the panic incited by the sound of a text notification during a period when one of my children was very unhappy at school. It's a chemical reaction ... an immediate rush of positive or negative emotion ... just based on a little sound coming from my phone. I'm on the alert, ready to respond. News stations are another example. Any bit of news is an "ALERT" to news stations. "ALERT, ALERT ..." they scroll at the bottom of the screen, "President Jones's shoelace is untied ... ALERT, ALERT" They want to have us constantly on alert so we'll keep watching. Our kids, too, are constantly on alert. They are always watching their social media for the next comment, the next response or the next message. For some it never ends, as their "alarm clock" (smartphone) is right at hand, next to them in the bed at night. (In our own family we encountered a problem with the delivery of peer drama to one of our children very late at night through texting. Because there was no internet access, we believed it was safe to allow the phone to be in our child's possession at night. Not so. We had to remove the phone from the bedroom in order to preserve some peace for sleep.)

There's no denying that social media has fundamentally changed the way that our kids interact with others. Some rarely ever use their phone to make a call, at least to anyone outside their family circles. It was extremely frustrating for me that my high school kids (who now range in age from 19-25) could have an urgent question or problem that could easily be solved with a quick conversation, and they wouldn't make the call. Our interactions went something like this.

Me: "Why don't you call a classmate?"

Teen: "Well, I've already texted three people and they haven't answered yet." OR: "I emailed the teacher yesterday and I haven't heard anything yet."

OR: "They never pay attention to their texts."

OR: "He never answers his cell."

Me: "We have their home numbers in the school directory; just call them at home."

Teen: "I'll try texting again."

Me: "Just *call* the people."

Teen: "But I'd rather not ..."

Me: "***CALL* the people!**"

It was a complete disconnect. They talked to me on the phone; why were they so resistant to calling a peer or a mentor, teacher, or supervisor who had offered a telephone number to be used during approved hours? But today's kids prefer messaging, and they want to communicate with each other almost entirely through social media. They will sit together in the same room even, messaging one another or another friend who is not present with them. Dating is changed, with boys and girls often preferring, again, to sit in their bedrooms messaging one another rather than chat face to face or even talk on the telephone.

For some kids messaging is a substitute for real relationships, and they interact personally with others only as necessary. They don't know how to initiate or carry on a conversation. They don't know how to address a problem, make an apology, or ask somebody out (on a date) face to face. A guidance counselor friend of mine appreciated a teacher's observation that the greater breadth of communication enjoyed by today's students results in a shallower depth of communication. "Not only do students feel lonely and isolated," my friend said, "but they have the perception (often based upon the apparently happy, confident posts they see on other students' social media feeds) that they're the only one who feels that way." This generation craves authentic relationships but lacks an understanding for how to achieve them." This concern is echoed by parents who are concerned that their kids exist largely in the absence of true relational community.

Another very concerning aspect of social media is the ability of children to communicate anonymously or with complete strangers. In his February 2015 *Washington Examiner* article entitled, "Nine Most Dangerous Apps for Kids," Paul Bedard cites **Whisper,** an app that allows your child to "whisper" a secret (to chat), anonymously and non-selectively to any other users in her geographic area; **Yik Yak,** an app which allows (without creation of a profile or account)

anonymous commentary accessible to the nearest 500 users (within a limited range); and **ChatRoulette** and **Omegle,** which enable video chatting with strangers (*Washington Examiner*, Paul Bedard, Feb. 2015). Obviously internet chat rooms and social media accounts are methods by which kids can make contact with complete strangers. Many kids create accounts that their parents don't know about, often using a friend's device, gaming device, or even a library computer. Know too, that it is not unusual for other children to create a social media account for your child — either at your child's request or without your child's prior knowledge — either as a favor, a joke, or a malicious prank.

Younger Perspectives

When I queried each of my own post-high school young adults (who didn't even have social media accounts until 8th or 9th grade and no smartphone until senior year of high school at the earliest) about what they saw as the greatest challenges facing kids today, one of them cited the internet, and two had social media toward the top of their list. Appreciation was noted for the measures we took to hold our kids accountable with respect to internet use. With regard to balancing protection from the perils of messaging and social media against the teens' determination to maintain constant access, it was acknowledged that some compromise must be reached.

One of my young adults recounted having experienced considerable stress relating to the pressure always to be politically correct in every context including social media and noted that political correctness changes from community to community, such that one must be very careful. There was acknowledgement that, as we have already noted, "People will say anything about you online" (also true to a lesser extent with messaging applications).

Another noted problem was the tendency of our young people to identify with particular online labels and associate closely with electronic (virtual) subcultures. A quick look at the posts on any number of social media websites (Imgur) reveals radical changes in the way these groups communicate, each with its own iconographies, acronyms, and/ or language. "It can be best described as almost tribal." Wikipedia lists 56 internet subcultures, and these are only the tip of the iceberg. These can be as innocuous as Trekkie (Star Trek) or Rockabilly or as toxic as anorexia/bulimia (see https://www.ncbi.nlm.nih.gov/pmc/articles/PMC2901299/), white supremacy, and jihadism.

Teens, especially those who do not feel they fit in well with their school or community, seek online niches into which they will be readily accepted (or even create fictional identities in order to be accepted) and, having discovered such cultures, may identify very strongly with them. There are plenty of virtual subcultures eager to accept your children as adherents to their tenets, which are not necessarily correct or healthy. Many of these subcultures are populated, in fact, by other young people who do not have their own feet firmly on the ground, and who may do harm to one another even in their attempts to provide acceptance and support. It's not all bad; association with others through such a culture may help kids under certain circumstances, providing an outlet for self-expression and possibly mustering some support and positive affirmation, but it's a mixed bag. Because the internet connects us to people of all persuasions, it can also provide comfort to our internal enemies. We can find someone to encourage or excuse us in almost any behavior.

People who identify strongly with very narrow virtual subcultures can become unbalanced in their thinking. "Peer soup," it was called, since a given group is at least ostensibly homogenous in its ideologies, with little toleration of dissent. "Ideas take off much more quickly (due to social media peer connections) and don't have to make sense. Social acceptance of these ideas has outpaced the rate at which they can be tested in society." Individuals within a given subculture tend to affirm and not to challenge one another, such that any assertion may gain almost immediate approval, at least within the narrow virtual society.

Again it's my own observation that this can affect adults as well as kids and may be another explanation for the stark disunity we face in our country.

Chapter 5

Pressure

A very common source of stress reported by teens relates to pressures: social, academic, and athletic. I remember feeling pressures, both social and academic, as a teen. Overall I can honestly say that I didn't enjoy high school (although I was much happier in college). I was the kid who never had a boyfriend, never went on a date, and usually had to take potluck for roommates on band trips. It was partly of my own doing; I didn't extend myself well to others. Friends had to fall into my life; I didn't go out of my way to draw them in. I would have to say that in my world the social pressures outweighed the academic pressures. If I hadn't done so well academically, it might have been all the more difficult not really fitting in socially. But I had my family. A strong, supportive, imperfect family who loved me. It was enough to get me through.

When my kids talked about academic pressure I never could quite understand it. They all seemed to spend less time on homework and less time practicing their instruments (both individually and with the band) than did I. Two of them did have a 45-minute longer school day than did I (because they chose to take classes during the extra period), and they all took AP classes, which we didn't have at my school. But I, too, followed a pre-academic program with four years of math, science, and English.

One of my children complained much more about academic pressures than did the other two, although that child's performance was consistent with theirs. This must say something about personality. Certainly it must also vary from family to family, from school to school, and from community to community. But with so much talk about pressure there must be something. Or is it all talk? From my reading and the input of others, here's what I was able to gather.

Overcommitment

Kids are too busy. They need planners right out of the womb, it has been said. Their days are crammed with lessons and classes and playdates and camps and sports practices. It starts with Mozart in utero, "Mommy and Me" or "Daddy and Me" classes for babies, or maybe the "Your Baby Can Read" program. Sure, anything that a child enjoys together with his parent almost has to be a good thing; and we all want to do what we can to enable our child to develop to his or her full potential, but for parents could it be (even unwittingly) a competitive thing in which we are already trying to give our baby the jump on other children? Probably so.

It's too much, too early, experienced parents say. Kids, especially the athletes, are scheduled from dawn sometimes until late evening and even then may have yet to complete their homework. In defense of parents, it is generally good and healthy for *teens* to be fairly busy. The older the child, the more responsibility (whether toward school work, home and family, athletics or other extracurriculars, or work) he or she should be taking on. As the proverb goes, "Busy hands are happy hands." And where it's not safe for kids to run free, organized activities are a good answer. Still, many of us have erred on the side of too many and too much.

Many children have almost no free time. No downtime. No time for family dinner. No time for the grandparents. No time for household chores (probably even more important to development than lessons). No time for training at home in the things that are important to you and to your family. And no time for discipline. When you can't put your kid in "timeout" because there *is* no time, when you can't "ground" your teen anytime this week because he has to be at practice, it's too much. You have a problem!

I vowed it would not be that way in my family. My kids would not be forever running from here to there and there to here. Only one activity per child, I vowed. And it was, for a while, for the boys. But then there was church on Wednesday night. That couldn't be skipped, so really it was two. And a couple of futile trials with Upward Basketball for the oldest — but those were only for a short season during the winter. Then my older son wanted to join a scout troop, so we allowed that along with karate practice. Our young daughter ought to have an activity, I thought, and I enrolled her in gymnastics. Our second son wanted to join both gymnastics and scouts, and we didn't want to deny him those privileges. When my daughter, too, wanted to join scouts, we signed her up. Already we were busy, but it seemed only fair that she be allowed to participate in scouting like her brothers. So now we had "only" karate, gymnastics, scouting, and church.

That's during the year. During the summer it was a little more relaxed. Then there were only the trips to the beach or camping, family reunions, evenings at the pool, a week of summer camp, a futile trial with soccer camp, a very happily received chemistry camp, swimming lessons, and always, home math practice. I loved summer.

During the teen years, with scouting and choir and tennis and ensemble and musical theater and stage crew and violin and band and taekwondo and Bible Study Fellowship (cumulative for all kids over their high school years), things got busier and busier, and we were that family that often did not get to sit down to dinner all together. At times it was unavoidable. There were definitely days when I felt it. All the activity was detracting from the quality of life at home and from my ability to hold my children accountable for any responsibilities there. And it did affect my ability to discipline an errant child in the most effective and timely manner. It seemed I was always feeling that things were a little out of control.

So we don't want our children to be overly "involved." On the other hand, standard advice is that parents should expose their children to a wide variety of experiences in order to help them find their niche — an interest, an area in which they shine. And then there is the social aspect. I heard it from administrators and teachers. One of our school guidance counselors as well recently voiced her belief that both public and private middle and high school students almost need to be a part of some school-related activity (sport, musical group, club, etc.) in order to feel that they "fit in." Our kids did find some niches, and ours wasn't the busiest family around. (It seems to be much more difficult for athletic families.) Maybe we kept an acceptable balance. But know this: it is most certainly a balancing act, and many kids are clearly overcommitted.

What might we in our family more wisely have omitted? I can't say even now, though for my children free play at home might have done just as well as karate. Interestingly, when I ask my kids today about the relative value of the various activities in which they participated, they indicate that they might have eliminated some (but not nearly all) of the activities they themselves chose or defended as children. We have to remember that there are all kinds of justifications for choosing and even for maintaining an activity, but those may be negated when for some reason the activity does not develop into the kind of experience we expected it would be. We must remember, however, that the failure of an activity to live up to expectations does not necessarily imply the absence of valuable life experience to be gained.

Stressed for Success

Recent years have seen several well-documented suicide clusters in affluent communities including Alpine, Utah; Palo Alto, California; and Fairfax, Virginia, communities which seem to meet many of the preventive criteria, such as affluence, family involvement, religiosity, and community cohesion. But as Jessie Hyde revealed in her article of December 2016 entitled, "The Lone Peak Story," research indicates the possibility of increased risk for teens in such cultures. "The study focused on a homogenous, upper middle-class community that experienced several suicide clusters and found that teenagers there faced intense pressure to succeed academically and conform to very narrowly defined standards of success," he says. The CDC reports similar findings in its studies of the clusters in Palo Alto and Fairfax. Lone Peak has in its employ a full-time therapist who saw 285 kids during the course of the year with significant anxiety and depression. "One student recently came into his office sobbing because she'd got her first A minus and worried she might not qualify for a certain scholarship. Another kid couldn't get out of bed for a week because he got a 33 on the ACT (36 is a perfect score)."

I could definitely see some kids in our community and school with such tendencies. Before I read it here I had made note of the same observation from my interview with one of my "children" in almost the exact same words: "Success is defined very narrowly."

In recent years I had heard similar comments about our school community from my own kids as well as from their peers (through the parents): "Here you have to be either pretty or smart or an athlete." "You have to be the best at something." "If you're not really smart or a cheerleader or a football player, you don't really fit in." These comments seem a little unrealistic, since not nearly all of our students are cheerleaders, football players, or geniuses (though we have had quite a number). It seemed incongruent as well that my student who said, "You have to be smart," though an honor student, felt decidedly excluded. It may be important to note, though, that two thirds to three quarters of the kids in our school are National Honor Society members. Those who fall outside the top fifth percentile seem to regard membership as little more than a rather questionably honorable mention.

Even if it does seem a little unreasonable for an honor student taking advanced classes at an excellent college-prep school to feel academically inadequate, we must remember that, in the minds of young people, **it is what it seems.** The social walls seen by many of the students are as real to them as the stone walls of your nearest fortress, and their perceptions of their own inadequacies, athletically, socially, and academically, are painfully real to them as well.

Jessie Hyde's article goes on to cite findings of Suniya Luthar, a professor at Arizona State who has researched the pressures perceived by teens in affluent communities. A study by Luthar revealed, basically, that the greater the parents' emphasis on achievement, the more troubled the teen. We always reminded our kids that their value did not come from their performance — that their value was, on the contrary, imputed to them by a God who loved them. That we too loved them regardless of what they did or didn't do. At the same time, we believed that education (and a reasonable degree of success in school) were critically important, and we always indicated that we expected of them what we knew they were able to do.

Did we, did I overestimate their abilities? Possibly. Not their intelligence, certainly, but perhaps their ability to perform. Maybe I wrongly assumed that their obvious intelligence should translate directly to performance in the classroom. Then again there were definitely those times when my prodding alone extracted an improved performance from my children. And it is not as if they were without help. We were there to assist almost anywhere they might need help. I have to believe that part of the pressure felt by my kids was caught, not taught. They were surrounded after all, by high-performing friends whom they chose for themselves. My kids seemed to be nerds, yet were not quite able to produce a nerd-worthy performance in school.

A journal by the previously mentioned Luthar entitled *Psychological Costs of Material Wealth,* dating back to 2003, provides a hint worthy of our complete attention. She notes that for children of affluence, "Successes are expected and failures are both highly visible and apparently inexplicable." What a shame it is both for the parents and child, people naturally tend to think, when someone who was perceived to have all the ability and all the opportunity does not seem to "perform" in life.

Luthar goes on to note the phenomenon that I observed in our school and at times among my own children, that "to be average is tantamount to having failed." The resulting stress, she says, presents as digestive distress, headaches, insomnia, anxiety, and depression. Luthar cites a statement by a B. Schwartz, in her article, "Self Determination: The Tyranny of Freedom," (January 2000): "The more we are allowed to be the masters of our fates in one domain of life after another, the more we expect to be ... In short, life is supposed to be perfect." When the expected perfection is not achieved under such circumstances, Schwartz notes, people tend to place the blame on personal rather than external causes.

As my guidance counselor friend noted, what we most often observe *outwardly* in our students is that blame for suboptimal performance is placed on any **but** personal causes: the school, the teacher, the test, the text, the schedule, anything else but "me." And for some students this outward observation may accurately reflect inward perceptions. But I believe that for most students the throwing of blame belies a sense of personal shortcoming being suffered (whether consciously or subconsciously) inwardly. If I believe the fault is mine, I may feel better about re-assigning it to you; and I may fool some. But, at least for the long term, I probably won't be able to fool myself.

So to simplify the point being made by Luthar and Schwartz, when parents themselves have been successful and are offering their children every opportunity, children may feel that they have no excuse for being average-ish. They should excel. Their parents are smart. Mom was homecoming queen, maybe, and dad was quarterback. The children go to the best school. They have the best tutor. They have the best coaches and have been trained since they were three. So if they can't measure up, well?

I think the above is key to the stress expressed by kids today. My parents were given little and made much of it. They wanted to give my brother and me "opportunities and experiences," including those that they themselves never had. My husband and I were given much and made something of it. We wanted our kids to have all of the opportunities that we ourselves had. Our kids were/are given even far more, by both their parents and grandparents. Materially yes, but also in terms of love and time and attention and experience and opportunity. So, whose fault is it if they do not produce? From their perspective, it might be enough to really give you the heebie-jeebies. No?

But, in our efforts as parents to give them love and time and attention and experiences, are we too focused on assuring their visible, measurable academic, athletic, and arts "successes" to provide the balance that will allow them to be truly successful? Do we want them to be successful in academics, athletics, and in the arts, or do we want them to be successful in life? Because the two are not the same. They do not equate either in quality or importance. Why are we so focused on our kids' "success" as the world defines it? Perhaps the visibility is a key. We all want our children to be successful, but is it for *them* that we want to see success? Or is it for *us*? We are working very hard to provide for them in every category, and what will be the visible measure of our success at the high calling of parenting? High grades, a stellar athletic performance, or some extraordinary talent would certainly do the trick!

We all have heard about parents who attempt to live vicariously through their children, who want their kids to demonstrate interest in what interests them —to reach the pinnacles that they themselves, never quite reached. I know that my husband and I tried to stay away from that. It's natural to want our children to share in our own interests and pursuits, and I'm not claiming that we never tried to sway them. Still we tried to recognize and respect their individual bents, and as they developed and specialized we have been able to embrace our kids' individual interests and directions. But there's a much more subliminal temptation for engaged parents for whom parenting is (very rightly) a high and sacred occupation, many of whom identify first and foremost as parents. The temptation is to seek validation through our children's performance as seen through the eyes of others around us.

Though I became vaguely aware of this tendency during my kids' growing-up years and tried to focus my attention on how my kids were developing — not how they were coming across — I know I stumbled at times. This is something about which today's parents need to be very, very careful. The goal of parenting is to provide the love and care and training that our kids need in order to become their best selves. We will talk more about the nature of true success in Part II of this book, but it is certainly not wrapped up in their grades or performances as children and teens. Those things, especially the academics, can be indicators, but as parents we must constantly remind ourselves that these are not the be all and the end all!

We must remember that our kids can see right through us, and whether or not they show it, they are desperate for our love and respect. They want us to love them and to be proud of them. If we say, *but cannot convince ourselves,* that their best — or their bent — is good enough, *they won't be convinced either*. For the sakes of our children it is critical that we fully embrace a right view of success for both our children and ourselves.

Part II Casting Anchor

"We have this (certain hope in an unchangeable God) **as a sure and steadfast anchor of the soul, a hope that enters into the inner place behind the curtain, where Jesus has gone as a forerunner on our behalf, having become a high priest forever after the order of Melchizedek."** — Hebrews 6:19-20, parenthetical added.

As we saw in Part I of this book, there are many senses in which the Selfie Generation is without anchor; unmoored. This is in no way a judgment against the generation itself. It's not a judgement at all. The purpose of the investigation is to identify, understand, and remedy underlying problems. Every generation struggles throughout every stage of life. This is the human condition. And the transition from childhood to adulthood has always been a pivotal and (for many) particularly turbulent phase of life. There are clear evidences of still greater challenges facing the Selfie generation however, including increases in depression, anxiety, suicide, and in some sectors, violence.

What is responsible for the unmooring of today's youth? We discussed many factors in Part I. But if underneath all of the currents and turbulence and winds and rain that buffet and batter our children there is a firm anchor, then our kids can be held fast. The absence of family stability, a void of faith, and a lack of consistent answers — these things leave kids without solid ground to stand on.

Our kids need something that is sure. They need people who are sure. They need rules that are sure. They need to know what to expect and what is expected of them. Conflicting or inconsistent beliefs and expectations make things difficult for a child. There should be a system underlying the rules; they must not be arbitrary. The underlying system must be respected not only by the child but also by the adults — by at least one important adult (hopefully a parent or guardian) in the child's life. If a guardian is not anchored but is himself riding the tide, not knowing which way to go ... even though he loves the child ... if he himself is drifting the child will drift as well.

So a child needs an anchor guardian, hopefully both Mom and Dad, but at least one who is himself solidly anchored in Christ.

Chapter 6

Family

Anchor. That intangible force that provides stability to our lives, that holds us against the storms of life: the cruelties, disappointments, betrayals, pressures, confusions. temptations, and failures. We all need this security, but too many kids don't have it. Ideally it's the native family Mom and Dad — the same mom and dad all the way through.

Realistically, and regardless of economic class, home is too often a tumultuous concept without clear form or boundary, always in danger of change. The traditional nuclear family is a rarity. Too many children grow up in single-parent families. Others must migrate back and forth between divorced parents. Then there is of course the blended family, and to further complicate matters there is the patchworked family, in which a parent and/or stepparent brings to the marriage children from multiple previous marriages. Many of our children don't really know where home is. They know only that they need it, they long for it, and it's gone. It's not there — not as it should be — for them. They get lost in the shuffle.

The ultimate anchor, of course, is our God and Creator; and we can have Him even in the absence of family or home. But the loss of the home makes everything harder, and when parents are preoccupied with their own, disrupted lives, they are not able to nurture and disciple their kids as they should. It's an arduous task even for parents who stay together.

Are there broken and blended and surrogate families who successfully serve as anchors for their children? Absolutely! Are there intact families who fail to provide this stability? Of course.

Are there children who, when faced with life's difficult challenges, may fail to thrive, even given an intact family and the presence of a solid and steady anchor in their lives? As desperately as I want to offer a resounding "No!" I have to answer, "Probably, yes." We are only human. And even the most sincere human effort is met with both successes and failures. In any case we must all do everything we can to anchor our youth. The challenge is to overcome our own self interests in order to put our children, our neighbors' children, and the children of our greater community first.

Marriage

Yes, we did already talk about family and marriage in Part I, in which we addressed problems faced by today's kids. But in the effort to prescribe some remedies to the problems, we must revisit the topic, and the first order of business is to address the singular importance of marriage to the well-being of our children. I am not overlooking the elephant in the room. It is not the purpose of this book to criticize or diminish families that do not fit the traditional "mom and dad" mold, and in the next section I will address the (more common) nontraditional family. But. since Mom and Dad are the origin of every child (in the preponderance of cases through the traditional means), we must address the parental relationship.

In the introduction to this book I disqualified myself as any kind of professional. Here as well I want to be very clear. I am neither a marriage nor family counselor nor a trained expert of any kind. What I present in this chapter, therefore, is common sense. The kind of wisdom that we already know, that is so clearly obvious and so timeless that we tend naturally to discount it or relegate it to obsolescence. It is truth that is elementally simple to comprehend and at the same time painfully difficult to fulfill, truth to which we really need only be awakened.

First, it is the responsibility of every potentially fertile person to assure that his or her children are conceived within the context of marriage. The fact that this is, to many, a very inconvenient responsibility makes it not the least bit less a valid one. A child is owed the opportunity to grow up loved and protected by his mother and father in the security of the knowledge that they are committed to the child and to one another.

But why marriage? Why wouldn't any firm, mutual commitment be enough? Theoretically it could be, but a contractual marriage provides a level of accountability that is not brought to bear on a more casual commitment. Holy matrimony is the ideal because sincerely regarded it makes us accountable not only to one another and to the law and any present witnesses but also to God Himself. In reality marriage commitments — even those forged through holy matrimony — are abdicated every day. This is a travesty. Still, a legal marriage makes the commitment more public, more binding, and more difficult to ignore.

As a woman and mother it is hard for me to understand why a woman would be willing to accept an informal commitment (or none) from a man before putting herself at risk of becoming mother to his children. It's not that I don't know the reasons and can't sympathize with them to some extent. Perhaps she is afraid this is the best commitment she can get. She is in love and cannot deny him for fear of losing him. Or she herself is unwilling either to commit to him or wait for someone else. Or there is no conscious decision at all but a spontaneous rushing in during a moment of passion. But, when she moves forward outside of the protection of marriage, she subjects herself to instability and risk, and not herself only but potentially her offspring as well. Regardless of her reasons, such a decision is not in the best interest of her children.

The story is little different for a potential father. Why would he want to risk losing his child (and his opportunity to father the child) to a woman who is not committed to him and to the parental relationship? Unfortunately, too many in our society (including women, at least until they find themselves mothers) are fixated more on sex and self than on our children. For as long as such a priority remains, we will have many, many children born to uncommitted or marginally committed parents who do not maintain their commitments to each other or fulfill their responsibilities to their offspring.

The above several paragraphs represent very simple, direct, straightforward, undeniable truths. But our society does everything possible — manufactures every convoluted argument — in order to work its way around them, for example:

> "It's my life, my body."

> "But, don't I deserve happiness?"

> "But, where is the responsibility of the father?"

Of course it's my body, and it's also my responsibility. And when I introduce a new life into the picture, the happiness of two lives is impacted. and I am responsible and accountable for one of them. And yes, the father is due exactly equal responsibility. But as mother it matters not at all whether my child's father is equally responsible — should he choose to abdicate that responsibility. So before children there should be a marriage: a public, contractual commitment which makes parents accountable to one another and to society for faithfulness to each other and to any children produced through the union. For the Christian this should be holy matrimony, a covenantal marriage making us accountable to Him to whom we all are ultimately answerable.

"But marriage is no shining example, with so many marriages unhappy or ending up in divorce!" may be the next objection. Sad, true, and irrelevant. The condition of marriages today is deplorable, but a marriage relationship, statistically speaking, is a far more healthy and stable alliance than a cohabiting relationship (thespruce.com, Stritof, April 2017). And people (including males) are not meant to migrate from relationship to relationship, least of all people who have children!

We have to recognize too that an unhappy marriage is not necessarily a hopeless marriage. That's what marriage is all about. Traditionally we have committed to one another for better or for worse, in sickness and in health, until death parts us. We are not going to be happy throughout the duration of that commitment. There will be days, weeks ... possibly even years ... when we are not happy. We may be unhappy largely because of circumstances external to the marriage, or we may be unhappy with one another. Yet we are committed. I am not suggesting here the toleration of criminal behavior or extramarital affairs (though under certain circumstances a marriage may be preserved even through these) or physical or malicious verbal abuse. But I am speaking of the natural human irritations, disagreements, and disappointments of almost every other nature. When we face these things, we are to persevere through hard times. We must seek God's wisdom, seek any necessary help, and do the hard work.

A couple of years ago my husband and I were out for an anniversary dinner. It was 30 years, but it was not a fancy outing. Still, our waitress asked whether this was a special occasion, and we owned up. In a little while she came back and said, "I hope you don't mind, but, since you've been married for 30 years, I wonder if you have any advice ... what is your secret?" No one had ever before presented us this question. I hadn't really thought about how to answer, and I didn't think my husband would be prepared, so I answered quickly, "He hasn't left me yet." It must have seemed a silly answer, but it was so very true. You see, I understand very well my own shortcomings as a wife. But he has never threatened to leave, has never intimated any such intention, and neither have I. It was decided long before we ever married that there would be no divorce.

When my daughter (who now says that she might like to become a lawyer) was about eight and first became aware of divorce through the experiences of classmates whose parents' marriages were dissolving, she became very concerned that her parents would be next. She came to me in the kitchen with a contract of her own design and informed me that, in order to prevent any possible divorce between her father and me, we were to sign her contract. I remember explaining to my daughter through veiled amusement that her contract was unnecessary, since her daddy and I were not at this time considering divorce, nor would we at any time in the future. I had forgotten all about this until recently when the following conversation took place.

Daughter: "I always hated it when you and Daddy argued. I was afraid you would get divorced. Remember when I brought you that contract I made?"

Me, laughing as I remembered: "I had almost forgotten. Did we sign it? I can't remember!"

Daughter: "Yes, you did."

Me: "Good. I thought we should have, but I just couldn't quite remember."

I'm especially blessed; I understand that. Not everyone enjoys the same security in marriage that I have enjoyed with my parents and husband. My 80-something parents and his, too, have been married for over 55 years. As we grew up our parents were faithful, supportive of one another and their children, productive, and active in our churches and communities. My dad helped in the kitchen after supper. He supported my mom in pursuing her master's degree and part-time teaching. During her seamstress years when she couldn't figure out how a difficult sewing pattern came together, he would help her. My mom tried to have supper every day at 5:15 when my dad returned from work and even have her hair combed and some lipstick on, but it was often he who fixed our toast or put out our cereal in the morning before school. Yes, they argued. My Dad tracks dirt into the house and drips water. My mom can be a little resolute, shall we say. But they always got over it, and we always knew they loved (and liked) each other. They still do. I knew what to look for.

ALERT! I'm going to say it now: Love is NOT enough. Not when "love" means only infatuation or attraction either to your intended or the perks or status that come with him or her or even the idea of being married. Love is not enough when you or your intended is irresponsible, selfish, unfaithful, untrustworthy, or lacking in self control. Love is not enough when I'm looking to see what's in it for me, when I need to make sure that I get "what I am due" from the relationship. Love is enough only when it comes with two-way commitment, the kind that is both sacrificial and persevering. The kind of love that is patient and kind, that is not jealous, egotistical or rude, that isn't selfish. The kind of love that always protects, hopes, trusts, and never gives up. (Okay, so it's not quite original to me.) None of us will be able to provide that kind of love — not perfectly. But it's the goal toward which we strive, toward which we *must* strive in our marriages. It's a goal, if pursued with determination and commitment, that will enable us to survive and thrive as a married couple, preserving a safe haven for our children.

When we're looking for our life's partner, therefore, we need to choose someone who is willing and able to give love that is sacrificial and persevering. We need to know him or her well and to see how she interacts with her friends, how he interacts with his family. We need to ask ourselves, "How well do I really know my intended? Does he share information freely? Do I know how she spends her time? Does he behave differently when he's with his friends? Does she withhold her friends from me? Is he respectful to his family and coworkers, even behind their backs? Is there a complete disclosure of life and experience, or do I note lurking secrets, discontinuities, voids in history, associations that I don't know about? Is there a willingness to work hard, to keep trying, to go the extra mile? Is there an outward focus, or is he or she really just looking to see 'what's in it for me?'" You may ask the same questions of yourself in order to determine whether you are ready for commitment.

We need to consider, too, how we operate as a team. Is our relationship centered only on us: pleasure and entertainment and comforts, or does it make room as well for others and for their needs? Do we both desire the same things in life? Do we agree on the basics regarding faith, family and family responsibilities, and finances? It's easy to overlook such things when we are attracted to someone and when it is just the two of us. "What's money," we may ask, "compared to love?" when in fact the way we earn and spend money reveals much about who we are and what we love. We may reason that differences of faith are not important as long as we love one another, but such little mole hills very quickly become mountains just as soon as a child is involved, if not before.

We may think, "We can work all these things out after the wedding," or even, "Things will naturally be better after we are married." This is rarely ever the case. As long as we are uncommitted, especially if deferring physical union, there is an incentive to be our best for one another. We want to look our best and be on our very best behavior. Soon after marriage or cohabitation begins, however, life begins to fall into a routine. We are no longer together only when we are at our best but early in the morning before work when there is no electricity or hot water and we have already called three times; when the roof leaks and water is flooding the house; when the dog is sick, or when we have had a bad day at work. In the everyday — or when we're harassed, grouchy, tired, and frustrated — we are not so highly motivated to be our best. Now that we've won the prize and sealed the deal; the earlier incentive is past. So we must choose our life's partner carefully, which requires that we know him or her well, in a great variety of contexts and circumstances, before making a commitment. And remember, commitment *before* children.

When "Mom-and-Dad" Is Not to Be

But what if the parents are irreconcilably divided? What if the divorce is final or the casual commitment and relationship are "over!" What if there never was a commitment; maybe it was all a big mistake. What if Mom or Dad passed away or is imprisoned or has abandoned the family, even in the case in which divorce has not been pursued? What if Mom or Dad is on drugs, and you, as grandparent, aunt, uncle, or neighbor, are taking care of the child(ren)? What if you are the single parent of a child by some means of adoption or you are the lesbian or gay parent of a biological or adopted child? If I believe that "Mom-n-Dad" is a critical need of every child, what could I possibly have to say to you?

To such parents I say this (which is no different to what I would say to any parent): Put your child(ren) first. I didn't always, not in every consideration, not in every moment of every day. I, too, had "other things" I wanted from life. Even in a monogamous marital relationship, even as an "at home" mom, I am not the poster parent. We're all frail, flawed, and failing. Nevertheless, this is the most important thing. You are obligated to the child that you have brought into the world. You may also have chosen to obligate yourself to a child that you yourself did not bring into the world.

Put your child's needs first. I am not talking short term. If you haven't eaten since breakfast and your child wants you to read her a story and cannot be patient while you grab a quick bite of dinner, require her to wait for a few minutes. By making her wait, you are sustaining the health of her parent and teaching her how to delay gratification. But we can't take it too far. There are wants (and lesser needs) we must forego because they are not in the best interest of the child. When it comes to the wants, especially for the single parent, it may be very rare that we can "have our cake, and eat it, too."

If you are divorced or separated from your child's parent and he or she is willing and able to invest in the child, if it seems likely that there could exist a relationship between them that would be beneficial to the child, then do all that you can to encourage that relationship. If you should find yourself contemplating marriage, follow the rules mentioned in the previous section regarding the selection of a life partner and then ask yourself in addition, "Is a relationship with this person in the *best interest* of my child?" because oftentimes it just isn't. If you've forged an unconventional family or a new family in the absence of your child's other parent hopefully it's good. You have to start where you are. Many a stepparent has substituted very effectively for a biological father or mother. In any case you must do the best you can *for the long term*, not primarily for yourself, but *for any children involved*.

If you're parenting alone, you're going to need some help. If grandparents are available and can be of support to you and your child, do all you can to nurture such a relationship. If grandparents or some other supportive family are not available, cultivate mutually supportive friendships with other parents so you can help each other in time of need. We all need family, and if we don't have family, we must make and be family. This requires care and patience, but we must do it nevertheless. There are many people who are willing to extend their families so as to include others, and there are also many people who need "extended" family, just as you do.

Watch for opportunities for your child to observe and know other families, traditional as well as nontraditional. If your pre-adolescent daughter has no mother, aunt, or grandmother involved in her life, be intentional about helping her to forge a connection with a female family friend, maybe a peer's mother. Don't be afraid to ask directly (not expecting, just inquiring) whether she might include your child with her own in some activities. When it works out, find some way to reciprocate, and have your child reciprocate as well (maybe a note or small gift). If your pre-adolescent son has no father, grandfather, or uncle involved in his or her life, adopt a similar approach. Perhaps he can participate in activities with another boy and his father. Again, be slow and careful in introducing other adults into your child's life. Study your child; watch and listen. Keep lines of communications open. Listen to your gut, and use your common sense.

Chapter 7

Faith

"My heart is in anguish within me; the terrors of death have fallen upon me.

Fear and trembling come upon me, and horror overwhelms me.

And I say, "Oh, that I had wings like a dove! I would fly away and be at rest;

yes, I would wander far away; I would lodge in the wilderness; *Selah*

I would hurry to find a shelter from the raging wind and tempest."

Cast your burden on the Lord, and he will sustain you;

He will never permit the righteous to be moved." — *Psalm 55:4-8, 22*

There are some hurts in life that cannot be soothed, at least for a time, even by those who love us best. The older we are, the truer this becomes. There comes a time when we recognize that our parents or family are not able to fix all of our problems — no matter how very much they would like to. So where can our kids go when neither we, nor their friends, nor their coaches or teachers or mentors are enough? And where can we go when our support system is not enough?

There is only One who is enough, all sufficient in every circumstance. Only in Him, ultimately, does any of us find anchor. It can all sound very cliché, very superficial, and yet it is truth in its very essence. "In repentance and rest is your salvation;" said the Sovereign Lord to His people in Isaiah 30:15, "in quietness and trust is your strength, but you would have none of it." How comforting this verse is but for the knowledge that sometimes I am the "you" who will "have none of" God's gracious and merciful plan for me. A believer, yet not willing to stand on belief; trusting Him for eternal salvation yet not willing to trust Him with the trials of today; knowing where He wants me, and at the same time determined to follow my own stubborn way.

But if as a parent I am not actively pursuing Him, how will my children trust Him? They are watching me. How can they believe that there is a God who loves and cares for them, who has their ultimate good at heart and who is there to preserve them through every storm, if I don't live as though it were true for me as well as for them? They may be young, they may be inexperienced, but they are not fools.

God is not just for little children, and, if we are using faith as a construct with which to pacify our children when they experience sadness or loss or to extract from them moral behavior, we are discrediting ourselves (as people of faith) and our faith completely. If we take them to Sunday School to learn faith as we take them to soccer practice to learn soccer, if we put them in Christian Schools in order to protect them or to give them a little dose of Bible or to make them "good" (at least while they are little and good is still cute) and do not live the faith ourselves —when we sit at home and when we drive upon the road, when we lie down and when we get up — we are discrediting ourselves and our faith completely. If it's not worth our fervent pursuit, it's not worth theirs either.

Another means by which we, even as committed believers, undercut our children's faith (and well-being) is through our preoccupations. Like our kids, we parents grew up in a culture that taught us to focus on ourselves, and too often that's just what we do. Too much of our time is spent on our own pursuits: making money or securing reputation, playing golf or tennis, dating, or creating a beautiful home. If not that (or in addition to it) we are busy driving our kids everywhere: sports, cheerleading, gymnastics, ballet lessons, and tutoring — all aimed at least in part at helping our kids succeed. (I know; when asked during my kids' growing up years to specify my occupation, I always filled in the blank, "Road Mom.")

Success for kids, as defined in our culture, is measured primarily in academic, athletic, or creative performance. But why are we so intensely preoccupied with our kids' success, resulting in so much driving around? Because somewhere deep inside, we believe that their success in these areas is the evidence of ours, as parents. So while our focus is on them, it may not be *about* them as much as it is about us. We must carefully examine both our own motivations and our kids' individual needs. Otherwise it's easy for us to run all over our own kids in *our* pursuits of *their* success.

As believing parents we already know that success, according to the Creator, is not measured in academics or sports or artistic ability. We know this, that what the Lord requires is that we do justice, love kindness, and walk humbly with Him. We know that we are to love the Lord with all our hearts and all our minds and all our souls and all our strength and to love those around us as we love ourselves. We know that we are to remain in Christ and obey His commands. We all agree that these — the eternal things — are far more important than temporal things. And yet there is something in us that so wants the worldly successes for them as well. We and our children do have to live in this world, after all. And we all need to eat, right? So our children need to be well-educated or accomplished in some way, and they need to know how to handle themselves well in society, says our practical/material parental instinct.

Evidence hints that even when parents report the rightly ordered priorities for their children, their children are hearing that order in reverse. They are getting the message, loudly and clearly, that accomplishment and personal happiness come first. In her June 2014 article, "Why Kids Care More About Achievement Than Helping Others," Jessica Lahey reports on a Harvard University study investigating empathy in children. Study results showed that 96 percent of parents indicated a strong desire to cultivate empathy in their children and cited the development of empathy as "very important, if not essential" to their moral development. Kids (80 percent), on the other hand, reported that their parents "are more concerned about achievement or happiness than caring for others," she says. And 75 percent agreed with the statement: "My parents are prouder if I get good grades in my class than if I'm a caring community member in class and school."

Lahey's article includes a quote from Richard Weissbourd, one of the study authors, which is quite telling. "We were surprised ... to find how many youth value aspects of achievement over caring and fairness ... (and) by what seems to be a clear gap between what parents say they're prioritizing and the messages that youth are picking up ... We need to take a hard look at the messages we're sending to children about success versus concern for others and think about how we can send different messages."

Does God want us to educate our children? Yes. Does He want them to learn to work hard and pursue excellence? Yes. But in exactly which fields and how many? And how much excellence is enough? Because we know that they can't be perfect, any more than we are. From here then, we must tread very, very carefully. We mustn't use the above absolutes to justify pushing upon our kids our worldly, even selfish desires for their success. We need to interrogate ourselves. Does my child need this? If not, does my child want this, or is it only I who want it? And is this detracting from other, more important and lasting life priorities?

There is no end to the preoccupations we can find to distract us from our top priorities: sports leagues, social clubs, hobbies, even studies or volunteer work or ministry. As has often been said by a certain little-known author, "There's just so much great stuff to do!" If we're not very careful we'll let these great activities (or at least the sum of them) take time away from the development of our personal faith (time in personal prayer, worship, Bible study and meditation) and the discipleship of our children. And when parents are too busy with other things (though we ourselves are believers), we are not focused on living it out in front of and side by side with our kids. We've all heard it said that our kids don't learn by what we say but by what we do! We must therefore be consistent about the business of training our children, living by faith daily.

I feel somewhat hypocritical in writing all these things, because I know that I didn't always maintain the balance myself. I know that I didn't always put my children first. I know that in certain aspects I failed them. It feels a little unfair, therefore, to be demanding all these things of parents just *after* my youngest escaped the age range about which we are talking here.

What I am trying to say here is that I *know* it isn't as easy as it sounds like it should be. I know that while you are trying to raise your children, there are a million thoughts and responsibilities whirling around in your mind, and you can hardly get to discipling them for cleaning spills off the floor, filling out paperwork, answering texts from school, and running back and forth and back and forth and back and forth. I know that, at least at times, you *have no choice* but to teach on the run and train on the run and sometimes even discipline on the run. I know how it feels to look at the papers displayed in the halls at school and be jealous of the beautiful paper of another mother's child, how it feels to have a child who lags behind the others in some areas of development and to see him hurting when it's clear that he doesn't measure up. I know that it's not entirely selfish. You want it for them *and* for you! And I *know* that there are those times, too, when all you really care about is getting to the place where you can get some sleep or just have a few moments of peace. I *know*.

But we have to try. I had to write the book, because it is the outpouring of my observations and concerns and heartache for our kids and because we must try, always, to come more in line with where God would have us as parents. And some of the specifics may not apply to me as a parent of grown children, but the principles do. And it is still hard, but I have to do my best.

I'm not claiming that if we were to do everything right (which we cannot) our children wouldn't struggle. Or that those who trust in Christ won't struggle. Obviously they can and do — some have chosen to end it all. Somehow their quiet desperation overtook them, and, though they had trusted Christ for their eternal salvation, they could not trust Him in the moment. They were so completely overwhelmed that disappointment or fear or guilt or shame ... at least for the moment ... outweighed faith, and from a dark valley which might have been crossed in only a short time, they took the escape route. Perhaps in that moment they believed that heaven was the only hope left to them. Somewhere maybe communication failed —the children wouldn't talk because they were embarrassed or ashamed or just too depressed. Or maybe they talked, but their parents were preoccupied or overwhelmed and emotionally unable to acknowledge. In any case, these children just weren't able to take hold of the promise in such a way as to trust that tomorrow could be a better day.

Could something have been done differently? In the case of those who are lost to us, there is no point in wondering. We don't know; we can't know.

We must in simple, childlike faith commit them into His hands. But, for those who are yet with us, we must assume that there is something we can do. For our children and for the children around us, we must serve, in any way we can, as anchors — those who are reliably there, who care, and who are ourselves firmly anchored in Christ.

Chapter 8

The Making of an Anchor

What Does It Mean to Be an Anchor?

Very unfortunately, the birth of a baby does not automatically transform his parents into anchors. If only! While we as parents need to be anchors for our children, true anchoring requires commitment, humility, and work. Yes, in many ways our children are naturally tethered to us. But, as we have said before, if we're adrift, they are drifting as well. We must understand that we're accountable. That we exist is no accident. That we are parents is no accident. That we have been given the breath of life is no accident. We all feel it, that sense that there's a reason; there's a purpose; there's something more than what we can see, and there is an authority behind it all. We know, too, that there is something "wrong" with the world, and not only that, but there is something wrong in us. We know it somewhere deep, deep inside. We may ignore it; we may deny it for a time, but we know.

Just tonight a friend was telling a story (from many earlier in her life) about being in a canoe far out on a very large lake during a terrifying thunderstorm. In the boat were a total of three young adults, all thoroughly trained in atheism by their government/culture; but in their fear they prayed to God to save them. "We all were atheists," she said, laughing, "but we all prayed!"

"For what can be known about God is plain to (us), **because God has shown it to** (us). **For his invisible attributes, namely,**

his eternal power and divine nature, have been clearly perceived, ever since the creation of the world, in the things that have been made. So (we) **are without excuse ..."** — *Romans 1:19-20*

Clearly, unless we ourselves are firmly grounded in our Creator and Sovereign, we cannot lead our children to that safe place. The first step then and one that must be refreshed moment by moment, is to right ourselves with respect to God. We must agree with Him about who we are with respect to Him. We must acknowledge His authority and our accountability to Him, His power and our weakness, His holiness and our unfitness. We must agree with him about our frailties, flaws, fears, and failures. He is a God of love and mercy, faithful to forgive when we ask Him. **He who did not spare his own Son, but gave him up for us all — how will he not also, along with him, graciously give us all things?** — *Romans 8:32*

In order to remain in a right attitude before Him, we must make time for Him, to listen to Him (Bible study) and communicate with Him (prayer). If we faithfully pursue the relationship that He desires to have with us, we will find Him to be for us that faithful anchor. We may not always *feel* anchored, but He has us. He tells us: **"I know the plans I have for you ... plans for welfare and not for evil, to give you a future and a hope. Then you will call upon me and come and pray to me, and I will hear you. You will seek me and find me, when you seek me with all your heart."** — *Jeremiah 29:11-13*

Ultimately both we and our children need to be anchored in Him. No other foundation is able to withstand all of the storms and battles that we will face. He is able not only to hold us, but to give us strength and wisdom for the anchoring of our children.

"I will praise the Lord who counsels me — even at night my conscience instructs me. I keep the Lord in mind always. Because He is at my right hand, I will not be shaken."

— *Psalm 16:7-8*

It's not only a religion, not only a practice; it's a relationship. We may already know and say this. We may make all the right noises. But are we really there? Because it's not about Sunday morning or Wednesday night or the good things that we are doing — not really. It's the whole of life. Do we live as if we know that He sees, that He is with us? Do we live as those who know that a debt is owed to the one who gave His own sinless life in order to bring us back from death? Do we call upon Him as though we know that He hears when we talk to Him?

We parents desperately need this kind of relationship with our God and Savior. And our kids need to watch us as we strive to live within it. It's okay if we fail. We can be forgiven. Even if we've never really even made it a priority, even if we were completely tuned out or have just been going through the motions — if we're ready to turn around. When I say it's okay, I don't mean it's good. I just mean that God always has a way forward. Maybe we've messed up royally. His love and forgiveness are there for us anyway. He is not surprised. He knows us better than we know ourselves; and He still loves us.

"The Lord is merciful and gracious, slow to anger and abounding in steadfast love.

He will not always chide, nor will he keep his anger forever. He does not deal with us according to our sins, nor repay us according to our iniquities. For as high as the heavens are above the earth, so great is his steadfast love toward those who fear him; as far as the east is from the west, so far does he remove our transgressions from us. As a father shows compassion to his children, so the Lord shows compassion to those who fear him. For he knows our frame; he remembers that we are dust." — Psalm 103:8-14

In the Storm

"Not only that, but we also rejoice in our sufferings, because we know that suffering produces perseverance; perseverance, character; and character, hope. And hope does not disappoint us, because God has poured out His love into our hearts through the Holy Spirit, whom He has given us." — *Romans 5:3-5*

So what do we do when we've messed up? We own up to it, and we turn. No matter how many times we fail, and we do *all* fail (yes, even believers), this option is still open to us. It is good that our children see us grappling with life, chasing after God, failing and then struggling to stand again. They learn from us how to walk, how to talk, how to live before God, and what to do when we fail. They need to see us taking our joys and griefs and concerns to God. They need to hear us bringing them, by name, before Him.

And what do we do when something goes wrong — maybe very wrong — with our son or daughter? We cling to God. We pray. We commit it all to Him: the disappointment, the hurt, the anger and the guilt. It's normal (to be expected even), that we should experience all the emotions; still we must commit our circumstances to Him. He is in control. He Himself knows and is the answer to these emotions. We walk the floors, maybe, but ultimately we must rest in Him, even in the midst of fear and heartache for our children.

An anchor doesn't panic. Panic responses include overwhelming anxiety, fear and anger, and none is helpful. I regret to say that there were times when I failed in this area. My panic wasn't over the top behaviorally. I was less likely to lash out or break down than to be switched immediately into a persisting mode of anxious hypervigilance. But my anxiety wasn't helpful to them. It finally occurred to me that this response to a pressing concern about a child was exactly the opposite of what my children needed. I began to pray and have others pray with me —especially when I felt anxiety building over one of my kids — that God would enable me to remain calm and collected in the midst of turmoil, a source of strength and shelter to my children. As a result, God is helping me to grow in this area.

Guilt can be another immediate reaction to a crisis with a child. My husband has a background in pediatric oncology, and he has observed that a parent's first response to a frightening diagnosis is often the feeling of guilt. A parent may immediately begin to wonder, "What did I do wrong?"

"But it's understandable," I said to him, reflecting on my own experience, "because as a parent you know for sure that you haven't gotten everything right!" He then went on to explain that parental guilt is not always entirely rational. Parents often feel the same guilt when the diagnosis is (at least as much as any can be) solely physiological, he said, and went on to describe to me his experience of revealing a diagnosis of cancer in a child (now happily cured). The mother immediately claimed the fault for the child's sickness, naming her own actions as causes. Of course, my husband quickly countered her reaction and assured her that she was in no way the cause of her child's disease. Still the experience is revealing of what we experience as parents when our kids struggle. When we do experience parental guilt, we must acknowledge it openly to God and to ourselves. If we find after some time and close examination that the guilt is well-placed, we may find it appropriate to acknowledge it before our older children as well.

Struggle and suffering are an integral part of life and one which is necessary to the development of faith and character in us as well as in our children. We must expect it; and when it comes, our part is to stand firm, anchored in Christ, so that we in turn can anchor them, guiding and supporting them through their trials with God's help.

Wisdom for Anchoring

As anchors we must understand that high intelligence, high accomplishment, and popularity should not be our top priorities for our children. Not only is the absence of these no disaster, but their presence brings unique and difficult challenges of their own. Look at the lives of famous young musical, acting, or athletic talents — those who made it big, early in life — and you will see that, in the economy of life, unbalanced talent and acclaim can come up woefully short and pose life challenges that are exceedingly difficult to overcome.

As anchors we must understand that there are critically important life lessons our kids need to learn from us, including humility, repentance, forgiveness, responsibility, hard work, and service to others and that by far the most effective way of teaching these is to practice them before and beside our children. We can't teach them by telling; we must teach by demonstrating and by providing valuable "hands-on" experience.

As anchors we must understand that our kids learn from failure. We have to allow them to fall and even struggle to stand again. We don't want them to see themselves as failures; but we do want them to understand that they *will fail* and that they *can recover* from failure. We must understand, too, that our kids have to take reasonable risks. Risk provides the opportunity for growth and for richness of life. It is not too extreme to say that there is no life, really, without risk. It is our nature and calling to protect our kids, but we must know, too, when to step away. These are two of the hardest lessons that actively engaged parents face. We so desperately want to protect our children, but, if we don't allow them any room at all for risk or failure, we insulate them also from opportunity to grow. This particular parental weakness has drawn considerable criticism in recent years.

Finally, as anchors we need to understand how important it is that we live our lives in front of our children. We need to be real with them, to cultivate in ourselves integrity and humility and transparency. They need to know that they can come to us and speak (not disrespectfully, but) openly. We should be to them an open book. Yes, there is some information that is not appropriate to share with them. Yes, we must have some degree of privacy and even offer our children some (age-appropriate) privacy, but our children should know who we are and where we are going with life. If our own kids can't know who we are, essentially, and where we are going, then there's most likely something in us that needs correction.

Did I get it right, this anchoring thing? Sometimes, yes and sometimes, no. I never really saw parenting in quite this way (as anchoring), until I began to organize my thoughts for the purpose of expressing the idea to others. I was so busy during my kids' formative years that I felt I hardly had time to reflect, much less organize, my thoughts into any understandable form. I hope that this concept of anchoring will be helpful to readers and to me as well.

Though no longer the parent of a teen I am still a parent after all, and, while some aspects of parenting may be stage-dependent, anchoring is applicable to every stage. As long as you're a parent or are nurturing a child or younger person, it's never too late.

75

Chapter 9

What Else Can I Do?

Beyond positioning ourselves as firm and functional anchors for our children (which is by far the most important thing), what can we do to address more directly some of the problems identified in Part I of this book which pose such difficult challenges to our youth? In this chapter we will briefly address items not already covered in Part II. These are complex problems whose solutions are far beyond the scope of this book, but there are some things we can say — some measures that we can take — in order to intervene on behalf of our young people.

Violence and Poverty

What can we do?

1) Make an effort to address specific practical material needs that you see in your own immediate community. Is there a child in your child's class who has observable needs? Or maybe it's a neighbor or the child of a service provider that you use (or see) regularly.

2) Join in or head up efforts in your church or community to assist those in your greater community who have material needs. First, give generously of your financial support to such efforts. Reputable organizations who have time and experience invested in their

ministries are able to help the many needy who may live unseen beyond the range of our own daily routes more efficiently than can we as individuals. Practice good stewardship. Investigate before you give so that you know that those to whom you entrust the money God has given you will make good use of it. Next, get involved *physically*. We are to offer our *bodies* (Romans 8:12) so whether it's fundraising or letter writing, sewing or cooking, construction or painting, whatever it is, do something! When we are unwilling to leave the comfort of our own little world in order to bring hope into someone else's, something is wrong. The problem of poverty is never ending; but every little bit helps, and when we work together we can accomplish great things.

3) Pay particular attention to the needs of children. What can you do for disadvantaged schools in your community in order to provide better care and education for the children there? Tutoring? Mentoring? Fun activities for the after-care program? Helping to raise funds for a better playground or to plant a community garden? What can we do to keep such children from believing that they are left to their own with no one even seeing or caring? I know that my gut reaction when I began hearing about the backpack food programs was anger and indignation. "What do you mean they *don't have food*? Can't people even provide food for their children? Don't we have government programs for that?" While some degree of indignation might not be entirely unjustified, I have to remember that:

> 1) I am not reacting from a place of knowledge. I do not know the individual situations. I have never had to rely on a government program for food, and I don't know how it works.
>
> 2) If a child does not have food, the first response should always be to provide it. Only after feeding the child can we appropriately ask, where is the fault? Why doesn't the child have food?

Because regardless of why a child does not have food, the fact remains that he or she is hungry. And a hungry child can do little else but survive.

We must do what we can to prevent any child from growing up hungry, hopeless, desperate, and alone. We see it in some of our teens and young adults: in the dragging feet, dropped head, and (in the rare moment in which they make eye contact) that look of complete deadness in their eyes. It is because they've been disappointed so many times that they've given up hope. They're lost, maybe angry, maybe too far gone even to be angry. In a sense they *are* the walking dead. Our goal, by any means possible, should be to eradicate this hopelessness in our young people, to come alongside before it ever gets to this point, bringing help and hope.

I heard a simple but powerful statement one time, I believe from a speaker on the radio, and I don't know to whom to credit it. But it rings so true to me from my experiences of being served by others in times of need, and I want to share it. His statement, which should serve as inspiration to each of us, was, "When we serve others, we give them hope." Whom can you serve? To whom can you bring hope?

Though I have served as mentor to underprivileged, inner-city youth in the past and my husband and I have sponsored overseas children throughout our marriage, I don't work directly with children in my community just now (having more recently been involved in service to the elderly and non-native in our area). But maybe you can! One person can't do everything all the time, but each of us can be doing something, somewhere, during most every season of our lives.

4) When you vote, carefully consider the issues and vote for the good of the greater community, not only for your own good. The issues surrounding poverty and violence are complex and difficult, and sometimes it is hard to know which approach is right. We, even those who are believers, will not always agree. Be sure that you are not voting only to benefit yourself and your own but that you are voting for what you believe is best for the whole. Try, when you are considering an issue, to place yourself in the position of those who

take the other side and see whether there isn't some merit to what they have to say. Our news media take very extreme positions to one or the other side of an issue in order to (appease their own viewerships, of course, and to) paint their preferred solution as wholly good and the opposite as wholly evil. In general neither is true. There are pros and cons to every party, person, and policy. Somehow we must rise above it in our considerations and make every effort see both sides of an issue and make a good, solid judgment.

5) Foster a child, adopt a child, or support the provision of care to displaced children in some other way. I know that there are opportunities to support, assist, or love children awaiting adoption or fostering as well as opportunities to support fostering parents. Lifesong for Orphans and (a branch of that same organization) and The Forgotten Initiative concentrate in this kind of work, and surely there must be many others as well.

One of our children is adopted. The path that led us to adoption was long and somewhat winding, but, long before I ever came to the point of serious considerations about children, I remember thinking to myself, "After two, perhaps it might be good to provide a home to a child who does not have one." It's no magic formula, and I'm not attempting to say that it's right for everyone. But, since there are always children needing a home/family, why not help them in whatever way we can?

Exploitation of Tolerance

NOTE: The goal of this section is not so much to prescribe a remedy for the cultural climate as to suggest how we might model and teach our children a correct approach toward others (which, if we do well, should have some desired effect on the cultural climate of the future world). This requires, of course, that we practice tolerance in its purest form.

It does not, as we discussed in Part I, require that we accept and laud every course or behavior but that we practice true respect and compassion for others, even though they are different. We want our children to be discerning — to know and distinguish right from wrong, but every bit as important is the cultivation of true grace, humility, and compassion.

What can we do?

1) Make every effort to love people wherever you go, whether or not you know them, whether or not they look like you, whether or not they look as though they like would agree with you. This is the right thing to do, and your children need to see you doing it. Look people in the eye. If they have a nametag, call them by name. Ask how they're doing as if you really want to know or even better, inquire more specifically. In the morning ask, "Is your day off to a good start?" or later in the day, "Have things been busy here today?" Note anything in common in order to start up a little personal conversation. If a service provider is on top of things, say, "Wow, you're really moving things along today. Thank you! How long have you been working here?" (and then write a review or tell the manager). Assign value to every person you meet, and treat them accordingly.

2) Don't judge people for things that don't really matter. Avoid criticizing people or making assumptions about them because of their clothing or outward appearance (within reason) and especially within hearing of your children who may not be able to distinguish concern or simple distaste from personal judgement. Don't judge a church on its music or decorations or any other style factor unless it clearly reveals some substantial underlying problem.

3) Don't expect unbelievers to behave as believers. If they don't believe, our calling is to win them with love, not to judge them for the evidences of their unbelief. I am not saying here that we have to embrace what is wrong or call it right. I am saying only that we ought not to expect an unbeliever to behave as if he believes. If he sins because of his unbelief, we ought, rather than to point and scold at him for his sin, to try to win him to Christ.

4) Don't accuse others without acknowledging first your own flaws and failings. Approach any necessary judgment with humility.

5) Don't be afraid in any context to objectively state objective truth. As believers we are to *speak the truth in love*. We are also to be prepared to answer anyone who asks us to *give a reason* for the hope that is in us, *yet we are to do it with gentleness and respect*, (not with our pointed finger and curled lip.)

6) Always remember that sin is sin. In Chapter 1 of the book of Romans, Paul gives a summary of the outworking of sin in fallen man. Idolatry is the beginning, then dishonorable passions, then evil, covetousness, malice, envy, murder, strife, deceit, maliciousness, gossip, slander, hatred of God, insolence, haughtiness, boastfulness, invention of evil, disobedience to parents, foolishness, faithlessness, heartlessness, ruthlessness. Paul ends here, noting **"Though they know God's righteous decree that those who practice such things deserve to die, they not only do them but give approval to those who practice them."** *--Romans 1:32*. Obviously he refers to all of the above listed sins, not just a choice sin that we as a culture or subculture have chosen to escalate to the pinnacle. So, we needn't think that someone else's sin makes him or her more unfit in God's eyes than we. Have we never been faithless, foolish, insolent, deceitful, malicious, or gossipy? Have we never idolized anything or anyone but God? As Paul says in Romans 3:23, **all have sinned and fall short of the glory of God.** But he goes on: (all who will receive it) **are justified by his grace as a gift, through the redemption that is in Christ Jesus.** *--Romans 3:24*. And from *Ephesians 2:8-9*, **And this is not your own doing; it is the gift of God, not a result of works, so that no one may boast.** Receive others graciously, as He has received you.

7) Love your children unconditionally. When my children were tiny, I said to them over and over again, usually at bedtime, "I will always,

always love you." I wanted them to be secure in that. It's so easy to say when they're little; and it is so critical, though it may at times be harder, to continue saying it to them when they're big. I was chatting recently with an elderly friend and several of his companions, one of whom introduced himself as my friend's brother. The brother seemed pleasant enough, but it made me very uncomfortable when he began to intimate, in the presence of my friend, how much better a sibling he himself was by comparison. I turned and looked inquiringly at my friend, who responded with a shrug and a nod, so I thought, "Perhaps it might be somewhat justified." But then the brother went on to tell me what a no-good their father was and then how many wives he (the brother) had been through. Finally he told me about his worthless son.

I'm sure that my friend's brother had probably suffered great disappointment because of their father's abandonment, but I wonder how much suffering he, in turn, may have caused by abandoning those who depended upon him. Even if my sibling had done me wrong, I would not have announced it to a complete stranger, nor would I have said of my son what he said of his, even if there were some truth to it. We don't have to accept or facilitate the wrong things our children do, but we should love them. We may not be "feeling the love," but we are to live out the love. This is our calling.

8) Expect your kids, during the adolescent and teen years, to question every bit of wisdom and common-sense advice that you have ever attempted to impart to them. OK, perhaps I'm exaggerating slightly. But, as you may or may not remember, we do come to an age at which we have to evaluate and decide *for ourselves*. It's a part of growing up, and we all do it to some extent. Today we have the added challenge of having to compete with a culture and subcultures that urgently press upon our children values which are completely backward. Don't panic. Don't try to force them to agree with you. Listen to them. Ask them questions to encourage them to think things through more completely. Discuss with civility. Give reasons

for your own conclusions. Give them time. Pray for them, and let God work it in them. Repeat.

Happiness Priority

What can we do?

1) It is right that we make our child a top priority. It is often taught that our top three priorities are to be: God, spouse, and then children. There is a very real sense in which this is true. We owe ourselves first to God, because we are His and then to our spouse, because we promised. But, when there are children, the children are the priority of the parents. The husband and wife together owe their combined allegiance first to God and then to children, in some circumstances possibly even to parents. Together we have to put our children's needs before our own. So children are in some ways, at least while they are young, at second priority. The problem comes when we roll not only our children's needs but all of their *wants and momentary happiness* into that priority or when our attention is not only upon what they needs from us, but also *what we need from them*. Each of these is an inappropriate attention, and each is detrimental to the relationship and to the child.

2) Meet your children's needs and some, not nearly all, of their wants, especially when it comes to material things. Do not try to keep them happy at all times. Temporal happiness does not equal a rich life and lasting joy. We all are unhappy when we do not get what we want, and yet we know that many of the things we want we are far better off not having. When we let most of our children's wants go unmet, they learn not to expect everything that they want in life. They learn that they are OK, even if they do not get what they want. They learn to be resourceful. When we meet every want, they are denied the possibility of learning any of these things. Instead they learn that they are owed everything that they want and that it is "only right" that they have it.

3) Examine your motivations toward your child to determine whether you are relying (or hoping to rely) on him to meet your needs. This is inappropriate. We are to meet the child's needs and not the other way around. Certainly he should contribute toward the well-being of the family as he is able. Certainly he should learn to be respectful and to exercise love and care for his family and for others. But he must not be expected to bring us accolades or acceptance or affirmation or to validate us in some way. If you detect in yourself such motivations, let them go. Parent your child; don't ask him to parent you.

4) At its heart this item is the same as the one above. It's not original to me; probably we have all heard it many times. We are to be our child's parent (or teacher or coach or mentor), not his friend. It sounds harsh. Are we not to be friends to the children we serve? Certainly, we are. But we are not to be peers. We are to be, first and foremost, parents (teachers, coaches, mentors) and only within the context of those relationships, also friends. There is a distance, not of relationship but of position, that is to be maintained. Just as God is higher than we, we are (not better but) higher than our children. It is not the same — no, not at all — because He is righteous, while we are not. But we are responsible for our children, just as God is responsible for us. And, while we are responsible for them, they must be accountable to us. We must reject the role of peer and maintain an appropriate position of authority that is ours not because of who we are, but because of our role in their lives. Certainly we should make every effort to be the kind of people who actually *deserve* our children's respect and the authority that has been entrusted to us.

Teachers, coaches, youth leaders, please note that the above refers to you as well as to

parents. Don't treat your middle or high school students/athletes as peers. In my experience, it is not uncommon to see teachers, especially young, male teachers, seeking acceptance, affirmation, and community from their students. This is inappropriate. It compromises your teaching, and since as a peer you will

naturally prefer some students over others, it can be very hurtful. To be clear, the most *popular* teacher is almost never the *best* teacher. Again, be a friend, but maintain appropriate separation. Do *not* try to be a peer.

Entitlement

In Part I, I mentioned two things that I believe contribute to the attitude of entitlement that we see in our youth and culture today: the happiness priority of many of today's parents and a changed perception of rights. We just addressed the first of these in the previous section.

In addressing the second of the two, I believe that we must first tackle the thinking of many parents, for we, too, are a part of it. I think that we all agree on the basic rights: life, liberty, and *the pursuit of happiness*. But somewhere along the line have we come to believe that it reads, instead, "life, liberty, and *happiness*"? Happiness can include many things: an easy life, plenty of money, a nice car or home that expresses who I am, a luxurious vacation, the privilege of pursuing any desire without judgment or consequence ... It can go on and on.

Do you think that it is the job of your spouse, coworkers, supervisor, or supervisees always to accommodate your will and ways? Do you feel like you need or even deserve only the best? Do you fail to notice and acknowledge the things that people do for you, even everyday things like fixing your meals, working to support the family, washing your dishes, doing your laundry, teaching or caring for your children, or maintaining your car? Do you talk down to or overlook the people who serve you, such as cashiers, waiters, custodians, or mechanics? Do you think that you are too busy or too important to take time for them? Do you tend to think that other people on the road or at the grocery or standing in the hall are always in your way? Do you think that all are stupid except (of course) for you?

Do you see any unjustified entitlement in your thinking? Even a hint of it? If so, that's a good place to start. Bring it under control such that your child sees a parent who is responsible for his or her own happiness, who does not expect always to be served by others, but who is willing even to serve others. Because if there is any entitlement to happiness, the next person is every bit as entitled to it as am I.

Having gotten this war against entitlement underway in your own life, you are ready to develop a strategy for your child.

1) Again, reject the urge to supply your child's every want.

2) Help your child understand that every sibling is equally deserving. They are not the same, and they will not be given exactly the same things or privileges or responsibilities; but they will be given equal love, respect, and consideration.

3) Do your very best, when your child is in any way competitive with others (whether in a disagreement, a game, an audition, a contest, whatever it may be), to see the other child in a favorable light, at least equal with your own. Help your child to see his peer equitably.

4) Require that your children thank others, as soon as they are able, for what others do for them. As they get older you can give them freedom about how they express their thanks, but do require them to express it. If you see that they are not showing proper gratitude to grandparents or other true patrons, withhold the gifts and privileges until the problem is corrected. Do not let them "work" their grandparents.

5) Do not run blindly to defend your child when there is a disagreement with a teacher or other authority. Do not ignore his complaint, but handle it diplomatically. Speak to the authority first. Understand both sides. Sometimes a child will misunderstand or exaggerate.

Sometimes, in fact, after time has passed, the child himself will seem surprised that you recount an incident with such drama (the same drama he presented to you) and will assert that it was, after all, no big deal.

6) Do not make a habit of buying only the top or most popular brands or shopping in the high-end stores or replacing your car as soon as it no longer smells new.

7) Require your children to help with menial household chores. Engage them in assistance to others when possible. Ask your child to hold the door for the elderly. If you see that an elderly person has dropped something, ask your child to pick it up for him or her. If a classmate seems to be dangling (always on the outskirts of the social scene) encourage your child to make overtures.

8) Offer your older children extra jobs, beyond their expected chores, for which they can earn spending money. Make them use their own money to buy gasoline, to pay for entertainment or lunch out with their friends, or to make purchases that you approve but do not wish to fund.

9) Do not let your kids get so busy that there is not time for chores.

10) Require "gainful" activity during the summer. Unless sports or education prevents it, your teen or young adult, age 15 or older, should have regular summer work. If the child has a lot of free time after school, he or she should have an after-school job, either paid or volunteer.

11) Do not buy your child a new car for his or her 16th birthday, and do not let the grandparents do it, either. Allow her to borrow a family

car, or buy a used car. The car should not be in the child's name until he is paying for his insurance and car maintenance.

12) Apprise your older children early of your family economic limitations and prepare them for what they can expect in the way of a car or college education. Don't take out loans for their college educations, and, in general, discourage them from doing so.

Technology and Social Media

This battle is a particularly difficult one because it involves fighting against something which has both very positive and extremely detrimental impacts and which is integral to almost every activity of modern life, education, and business. There was a time when we could more realistically have taken away the telephone or computer. To do that today, at least in my community, is a near impossibility. Electronic entertainment and education is widely available to little children from the moment they can fix their eyes and begin to understand what it is that they are seeing. Our children's attention is trained on their gaming devices, videos, and their parents' smartphones from the time they are two years old. They're learning to use the computer as early as kindergarten, with computer keyboarding beginning in second or third grade. Many kids have smartphones by fourth grade or even younger, and some schools are requiring that students have their own tablet or laptop computer by sixth grade.

As soon as a parent takes away the computer, he or she hears, "but I need to get online to get my homework." And sometimes it's true. Some teachers don't write it on the board anymore. The students are expected to check the teacher's website. If we take the phone, our students will miss group texts about group projects or messages from coaches or church youth group leaders. And, because so many students have their own smartphones, teachers are beginning to assume and to make use of the technology. Students are beginning to hear from teachers in the classroom, "Class, take out your cell phones ..." How do we effectively oppose an enemy which is as well a productive tool necessary to everyday life?

I might, and not unreasonably, argue that this battle is never ending, ever-changing, expensive

(in terms of both parental time and involvement), and ultimately unwinnable. Most 13-year-olds know more about internet and computer technology than we do, after all. If they wants badly enough to access something, they will find a way.

At the same time, we must recognize that this is a battle worth fighting. The efforts to teach your children from a young age how to self-monitor, to hold them accountable for what they're doing online and to assure that they cannot destroy themselves with the tools we have given them is an ongoing and sometimes exhausting labor of love and one which is entirely necessary. Just telling them is not enough. We, and I believe especially dads, need to demonstrate that our children and their hearts and minds are so important to us that we are willing to do whatever we can to protect them and hold them accountable. We need to educate ourselves on an ongoing basis in the "latest" technology and trends, learn how we can best protect our children, and carry out the plans. There are resources for such education; there are parental controls and accountability applications. The exploration of these is left to the reader.

Following is a list of suggested guidelines for protecting our children.

1) Little children do not need to be fixed to devices. Withhold electronic devices from preschool children, even your phone, except for video chatting with Grandma and Grandpa. Yes, a device can be a good pacifier, but we need to find something else. For the most part our young children need to be engaged in interactions with human beings and with their world, not to be pacified. Limit screen time for preschoolers to an hour a day unless they are sick and unable to physically play. Choose content very, very carefully.

2) *Do not* allow connectable (with access to cable or internet) computers or TV in the children's bedrooms! Even *and especially* in the teen years!

3) Have a common area, such as the family room, for computer use.

4) Limit the internet hours for each child's device. There should be NO internet or smartphone access after a reasonable quiet hour at night. (Keep in mind that there may be unprotected wireless networks in other locations close to your home that your children can access.)

The smartphone should be left, at least at night, where the parents can see it. A friend told me that in their home they have a phone basket. When the kids come home, the phone goes in the basket. The kids can use the phone there, in that location, at any time (until bedtime, of course). They cannot remove the phone from that spot.

It's a great idea to have all connectable devices (phones, iPads, computers) kept in one place, even when in use. Maybe they could be laid out on a work table, or a shelf next to a work table, in the heart of the home. That way parents can easily check the location of devices. The great thing about this is that, while, yes, it is very inconvenient for the kids, it is very straightforward and extremely convenient for the parents (who are paying for the phones and service and don't want to see their kids so negatively affected as many — if not most — are by the technology). It is so hard, nearly impossible if you have several children, to keep up with which child is allowed what and when and to police it.

5) Discuss content with kids when it comes up, and talk about why some things are just not worthy to be consumed. I always ask:

    a) Is it true?
    b) Is it honorable?

c) Is it just?
d) Is it pure?
e) Is it lovely?
f) Is it gracious?
g) Is it excellent?
h) Is it worthy of praise?

Philippians 4:8 tells us that these are the things we are to "think on and do." My kids don't always fully appreciate this line of questioning. I believe that they feel that the approach has a little too much of a Pollyanna feel, that entertainment (movies, videos, music, etc.) can be a little less than Sunday Schoolish and still acceptable for the believer. But at least it always makes them think more deliberately about the entertainment they are considering.

6)   There is no — I repeat, NO — - reason for a child under the age of 13 to be watching a movie rated R by today's standards. Let's be clear. Many, if not most, R-rated movie are not actually fit even for adult viewing. My husband and I did not watch R-rated movies until our kids were 16 or 17 years old, and then sometimes we would allow them to watch something Dad-approved, *with Dad,* who is very choosy and uses Clearplay or Vidangel editing. I still don't watch R-rated movies.

I believe that one of the most important things we can do to prevent the damage that technology and social media are doing to our children is to join together as a community to produce protective actions. If the whole community is doing it, I, as a parent, can do it too. But, if nobody else is doing it, it is very hard for parents, without withdrawing to homeschooling, to effectively limit technology.

Perhaps your school might agree not to have internet use until eighth grade (in many communities kids have considerable supervised access at home, so they are not falling behind by not having it at school) and then to provide school-monitored and privilege-limited computers on campus so that kids do not have to be toting their own devices all over town.

Perhaps your school might disallow the use of smartphones at school and prescribe only specific media through which teachers and coaches will communicate with kids. (Yes, I know that they will sneak them into school/class anyway, but at least they wouldn't be forever hunched over them in class or in the lunchroom) Perhaps the teachers could consistently *write the homework assignment on the board before class* so that kids couldn't say (whether true or not), just after internet hours, "Well, I need to check again because my teacher said he'd post the essay question, and he hasn't done it yet."

Just a thought: Perhaps as a nation, we could begin rating websites as we do movies, such that it would be very easy to create filtering to limit our kids' access according to rating. The ratings could be associated with the type of content or recommended age group. Unrated sites could be withheld. This would be no small undertaking (maybe the ratings could be created by consensus on a public site like Wikipedia?), but it might provide a way to afford better protection for our kids while still accommodating "free speech."

How about a school offering stiff penalties for bad internet/ social media behavior within its community (bullying, hacking, cheating, posting of nude photos or sexually explicit material, etc.) and substantial rewards for anonymous reporting. (I don't know ... is that a good idea?)

A homeschool cooperative could agree to have computer use only at home. No computer at school, ever. Computer assignments would be completed at home under parental supervision.

I know that some will say that each of the above ideas is absolutely archaic: that it is not our place as parents to limit what our kids can see but instead to help them navigate through it all. That the free exchange of ideas is not to be compromised by censoring. I say that our children's health ought not be compromised by whatever garbage anyone, anywhere, wants to dish out for them. But I know that there are others better informed and more ingenious than I who can bring far better (and more technologically up-to-date) ideas to their immediate and greater communities. I hope that you will do so, because while it is our job as parents to do what we can to protect our own kids, we can do much better if we work on it together.

Physical Appearance and Sexualization

The emphasis on physical appearance and sex in our entertainment and culture are so very pervasive. How can we possibly oppose them in the raising of our children?

First, we should keep our own enhancements to a reasonable level. For each person, the comfort level may be a little different. But, if we are constantly on the lookout for our next clothing, makeup, or jewelry purchase, driving from hairstylist to nail spa to plastic surgeon, we are telling our kids that appearance is an extremely high priority. And, if as women we dress provocatively, we are telling our daughters and sons that a woman is valued primarily for her sexual attributes.

Second, we should keep our discussion of physical attractiveness and attributes to a minimum. If we are always commenting on the clothing or style choices of others, whether those around us or celebrities or actors and actresses; if we are always talking about how attractive — or unattractive — they are, we are telling our kids that appearance is very important.

Third, we should not place too much emphasis on the appearance of our kids. If we're always buying our kids clothes, whether they need them or not, because the clothes are "cute" and the buying is fun, we are telling our kids that appearance and materialism are very important. When we take hours and hours dressing our little girls, getting their hair just so, when we make-up their faces (even for a performance) before they ever start to school, we are telling them at that very young, impressionable age that their appearance is critically important. It's bad enough when they are teenagers, but, if we make sure, when our kids are no more than five or six years old, that they always have the "right" looks and the "right" brands (especially when the price of the brand is much higher than that of comparable products), we are telling them that their appearance is of great importance.

We don't need to tell them that appearance is important. The world is shouting it out loudly and clearly. As long as they are clean and dressed appropriately, especially when they are little, they are fine. It's understandable, too, if we are able, that we provide our school-aged kids some clothing, accessories, etc. that give them the opportunity to fit in among their peers. But our provision should be more practical than market-driven or even peer-driven.

As is the standard advice, we ought not comment on our child's weight outside of its relation to her health. And, if we refer to the weights of other people, that conversation, too, should relate only to health. We should never refer to them or to any of their peers as "fat," and we need to be very intentional about teaching them not to do it either. Some kids are more genetically prone to being overweight. It's not fair, but it's there. And it's hard enough without commentary from others. They need encouragement and inclusion, not ridicule or isolation. If your own child struggles to keep his or her weight down, it is best that the whole family together — or at least one parent with the child — eats a healthy diet which will be advantageous to the child.

We need to tell our children that they are beautiful or handsome. They always are to us, and, even though they know it doesn't carry as much weight coming from a parent or grandparent (or any other adult, really), they still love to hear us say it. It is good, too, to make our comments specific. Maybe say, "I love the way you have your hair today," or "I am just enjoying sitting here admiring your beautiful green eyes!" If we have a child who is constantly told by others how handsome/ beautiful he or she is, however, we might need to provide reminders that physical beauty is not the most important measure of a person and that it does not ensure true joy and fulfillment in life any more than the lack of it deters them.

It's good that we help our kids, especially girls, to select the clothing that is most becoming to them. Yes, a few girls could wear the proverbial potato sack and be cute in it, but others benefit from more strategic selections. I'm tall, and I know that my choices are somewhat limited. I know what looks good on me. But my daughter is — well, not tall — so we had to try on and learn what styles look best on her. We still enjoy looking together (for just a little while — she can't tolerate much shopping) to find something that is just right for her.

The sexualization of our kids from a young age is an even more difficult influence to overcome. As we mentioned in Part I, sexual content, messaging, and innuendo is everywhere. In order to avoid it, we would need move to an isolated cabin somewhere deep in the wilderness — No? Okay, probably we couldn't even avoid it in a cabin in the wilderness. So, what can we do?

We have to implement protective measures (against the negative influence of online "information" as discussed in our section on technology) and more importantly to message our kids loudly and credibly enough that our "voices" will drown out those that barrage them from every side. This requires a good example and a lot of very direct conversation.

It is worth mentioning that women are probably just as culpable in the sexualization of women and girls as are men and that mothers are often a primary force behind the promiscuous dress and behavior of their daughters.

As women in America, we are not helpless. On the whole, we ourselves determine how we will dress and behave. It is the desire for attention that drives it, and as a culture we often talk out of both sides of our mouths. We want to dress in a way that we know draws attention to our femininity, provoking reaction in the men around us, but we don't want the "wrong" man to notice.

Further, as a culture we defend nearly every kind of music, performance, and programming and dismiss any objections as closed-minded and obsolete. We view as acceptable the propagation of all manner of sexual content including every kind of treatment of women, and then when young people act out or a man harasses a woman in the marketplace we are shocked and dismayed? Really? Why is it fit for viewing and not for doing? The point here, to be precise, is that it is fit neither for the doing nor for the viewing!

Certainly a man, and not what he reads or views or even what someone is wearing, is responsible for his own behavior. But why do we think we can have it both ways? If adult men struggle with self control when it comes both to their viewing and their behavior, how can we expect a teen boy or young man who has been steeped in such content to control himself?

As we saw clearly demonstrated in the popular television program, *Toddlers and Tiaras*, many mothers begin grooming their daughters for the spotlight from the time they can stand, and there seem to be few lengths to which we will not go to get them there. Maybe it's cute when they're little, but it's certainly very unnecessary and perhaps not so cute, either, when you extrapolate it to its likely conclusion as the girls are coming of age.

Costuming for some other events, such as dance and gymnastics, realistically are not too far behind. At the risk of revealing that I am entirely irrelevant, I purchased shorty leotards for my daughter, and they were adorable on her. When she got a little older, she preferred a snug pair of shorts and slightly snug T-shirt that always stayed in place. And I don't want to get too carried away here, because I do recognize that cheerleading, like gymnastics, is a highly specialized and very physical athletic sport, but there are cheer and dance team outfits that are really cute without being so provocative — and others which are very clearly designed to tantalize.

Let little girls be little girls. Let children be children for as long as they can. Let their development and not media or the pressure of their parents or others guide their awareness of sexuality. Don't press or even encourage your young children to have "girlfriends" or "boyfriends." Let them be. If they have a special interest, probably they will tell you; and, if so, don't give it much attention, but help them keep it light.

Provide complete information on an as-needed basis. When they ask, "Where do babies come from?" provide an honest, age-appropriate answer. Improve the information as more questions come or as you become aware that it is "time." As your kids approach their adolescent years, information is necessary *even if they are not asking*. If they're not getting it from you, they are getting it from their peers or online. Don't talk only out of a book, but converse freely in the context of life. People go on dates, get pregnant, have babies. Your kids will encounter it in the extended family, in the movies, on TV, and in music. Talk about it.

Tell your kids that they should never feel pressured to do anything that makes them feel uncomfortable. It is okay to say *NO*, okay to *leave*. Teach them how to avoid putting themselves at risk. Always know where they are and with whom. When your young teens are away from you, ask them to text each time they change locations. For example, if they have the use of a car and are leaving school, unless they are just traveling home at the end of the day, they should text and let you know, as a courtesy (and in case you should need to know for any reason) where they are going. If they are out with others (without access to a car), tell them that they can call or text you at any time if they become uncomfortable, and you will come and get them.

Teach your children that popularity is evasive and very temporal and that bowing to pressure can lead them down a dead-end road. Begin teaching them very early that people who press them into anything that they feel is wrong or a violation of their conscience are *not* friends, at least not in that moment. Teach them early, as well, that decisions regarding drugs, alcohol, and sex should be made before they are ever faced with the circumstance so that they will already have their answer firmly in hand. A decision made under pressure is often not the best decision. Teach them that if others say, "It won't hurt you," they can reply, if they choose, "It won't help me, either." Teach them, though, that they do not owe any explanation; all they really have to say is, "No."

Pressure to Succeed

We have already intersected this topic at some length in the above sections, but we'll hit it one more time. Some of the pressure experienced by our kids comes from parents, coaches, and teachers who want to see our children succeed, and some of it is generated in the children themselves as they see the social advantages of superior performance, especially in academics and athletics.

How do we as the adults in their lives avoid applying too much pressure while at the same time encouraging them toward excellence? None of us, after all, wants our children to settle for mediocrity. The first key to keeping the proper balance may be getting over ourselves. We all want our kids to be talented, to be handsome, to excel at *something*. We all want our students and athletes to take highest honors. It's not the most admirable desire, not the most selfless, but it is a natural desire nevertheless. The problem lies in the reality that there are just not enough highest honors to go around. If our kids need highest honors to make us happy, then not many of us are going to be happy. And since it is just as natural for our kids to want to please us as it is for us to wish to see them excel, not many of them will be happy either. We shouldn't expect highest honors of them, only success in keeping with their individual abilities. So, we're going to need to keep it in check.

Extracurriculars

We can start with activities. They don't have to have so many. They don't have to have them so early.

I remember well the first time I experienced that feeling of pressure or competition regarding my children's activities. I was at the community gym with my two little sons, probably four and two, for kids' time. We had parent-supervised free play for an hour or two, and then we had a snack time together. It was free, and what a nice opportunity it was for a mother to get out with little children, especially in the winter! Usually, I spent some time with my older son, kicking the soccer ball back and forth in the gym while my little one sat in the stroller. Then I would get my younger son out, and the two would play with each other or sometimes with other children. Riding toys were provided and a little basketball goal which was, prophetically, of no interest whatsoever to our boys (nor was the soccer ball except when I was kicking with them), but most of all there was room to run.

Anyway, on this one particular day I found myself sitting after playtime in a circle on the floor with the other moms and their kids at snack time. Then I heard it. One mom turned and said to another, "Oh, we started 'Connor' in soccer last week!"

"Really?" replied the other mom excitedly. "Where did you start him? We were thinking about starting 'Alex,' too." The two began to discuss enthusiastically the various soccer opportunities in the area, and so the conversation went.

It hit me like a ton of bricks. 'Connor' was younger than my son, and not only that, but I was apparently remiss in my duties as mom, since I had neither considered the possibility of starting my son into soccer, nor was I even educated on any of the area soccer opportunities. I'm sure that I must have mentioned it that night to my husband, and we probably said, "There's no hurry on the soccer." But the seed had been planted, probably without any intention whatsoever. I felt the pressure. Maybe I was letting my child fall behind the others. After all, my husband had shared with me his belief that some degree of athletic proficiency was critical, socially, for boys! Perhaps my son ought already to have been playing soccer by age three or four.

In retrospect we were right to defer soccer. In fact, probably we might just as well have omitted any effort to involve our boys in team sports whatsoever. The various experiments into which we entered them when they were a little older revealed that neither was cut out for athletics, particularly team sports. Neither possessed the natural ability, let alone interest or competitive spirit necessary. An aside for the purpose of illustration: When my second son was in middle school I encouraged him to join the cross-country team. The coach was great with the kids and included any student who had interest. "What do you do in cross-country?" asked my son.

"Well, you practice running each day, and you try to increase your speed. Then you participate in meets, which are competitions where you see who can run the fastest," I explained.

His response? "What's the point?" So much for cross-country. (But then in college he chose to take a course in running and ran a very respectable first half-marathon. Go figure.)

Anyway, back to the situation at our community gym. Perhaps 'Connor' and 'Alex' were natural athletes; and participating on a soccer team may have been fun for them but probably not necessary at such a young age. And the schedule commitment can place stresses on the family.

So, what is the moral of this story? The moral is, do what makes sense for your child and family, and do not be moved by what everyone around you is doing with their kids. It wasn't the fault of the other two mothers that I felt pressed. It was my own fault. And while it is true that we need to expose our kids to a variety of experiences during the course of their growing-up years (most likely to include at least some peer activities, especially if your child is attending a traditional rather than homeschool), the sources and types of experiences can vary widely. Who is to say that an activity schedule boasting soccer and gymnastics and cheer team is better than a schedule including household chores, a weekly family service activity, and a weekly afternoon with Grandpa or Grandma (yes, even during middle and high school years)?

We do not have to do what other families are doing. Our children do not need to be doing what other children are doing. It is so easy for me to say in hindsight. We *do* need to give our children opportunities to connect with peers — especially during the middle and high school years; they need a "place" to "fit in." But we do not have to and should not necessarily be doing what others are doing. Remember, ideas about what we should be doing change with every generation. Do the best that you can for your children, given your own circumstances and the available opportunities, now!

Destressing Success

We need to be sure, when we talk to our children about success, that we are not telegraphing the message that they have not succeeded until they've outperformed most or all of their peers. We must realize, too, that if we send them to a more competitive school, their class ranking will likely be lower. The number and level of classes they take as well as the number of and time commitment for activities in which they participate will also affect their performance. So, while they may be capable of making an A in algebra, if they are also taking advanced chemistry, advanced English, and other academic courses along with a sport or several arts activities, the grade might be a B instead. Therefore we need to consider not only what we believe they are capable of doing but also the totality of their academic and activity load.

It is important that we congratulate our children for success when they're producing work that we believe is in keeping with their ability, not discounting a grade or performance because other students made a better one. We need not smother them with adulation, but we should affirm their efforts.

The pressure that kids place on themselves may be more difficult to combat. What more could we want in a child than the desire to produce good work and the work ethic to back it up? But, if you detect that your child is under too much pressure of his or her own making, it might be good to talk to the child about why it seems necessary to do so well in everything. You could say, "I would rather see you happy, healthy, and well rested with B's than stressed and exhausted all the time in order to make the A's. Another approach would be to suggest a lighter load: fewer classes, fewer AP classes, or one less after-school activity.

If your child is suffering from constant pressure and at the same time underperforming academically (especially if the academic performance is compromising his valuation of himself or his ability even to keep up with requirements for advancement from grade to grade) it is important to explore every alternative: individual education plan, tutoring, or elimination of extracurriculars or reduction to only one. Homeschool (at home), especially in younger grades, can relieve your children of the competitive classroom environment and allow them to receive any extra help needed. It will give you the flexibility to tackle their most difficult courses early in the day when they are well-rested, and it will simplify their schedules. More of their time can be dedicated to learning activities since they won't have to spend as much time in commuting, changing classes, announcements, fire drills, pep-rallies, study halls, etc. And you won't have to compete with other families for music or gymnastic or tennis lesson times in the afternoon or evening. You can probably schedule any lessons before 3 p.m.

The approach will be different for every family and child, but somehow we need to teach our children two things concurrently:

1) It is important (and for no one else as much as for you, yourself) that you give your best effort to your work.

2) You are loved and valued for who you are and not only for what you do.

A Word to Parents

We've talked about numerous factors that create problems for our kids today and have attempted to address how we might be able to help. There are some factors, such as drug and alcohol use (a whole topic unto itself), which we haven't directly addressed to this point because they are often secondary to factors already discussed. But there is one sometimes (but not always) secondary factor that I do what to address, because we probably do not talk about it enough, and that is the underestimation and undertreatment of mental/emotional/social dis-ease in kids.

Probably this paragraph finds you wondering why dis-ease is spelled here as it is. It's intentional. Because mental/emotional/social disease sounds scary and intimidating. But the word disease, in its simplest interpretation, just means discomfort. If your child is so significantly uncomfortable with himself or his circumstances, with her thoughts or emotions, that it is causing him or her to be depressed or anxious or to withdraw and isolate, professional help is indicated. The need for help may be very short-term, just until "ease" is restored, or it may need to be a long-term need. In either case, ongoing discomfort should not be ignored.

It is important to observe our children and teens, and when we see (or they tell us) that they are struggling, to respond. If we are not able in a relatively short period of time to see the angst relieved or if the angst is acute, we need to move to obtain outside help for them. The reality is, however, that both children and their parents can be very resistant to outside help.

Why? For kids it's because they are trying so hard to be "grown up," to appear strong and happy, like everything is great and they have it all together. They want to stand on their own two feet. Who wouldn't? They may see pursuit of help as an acknowledgement of weakness; and, if not, they perceive that their peers would see it that way. Add to all this the likelihood that they have heard other kids (maybe even kids who themselves are getting help and don't want anyone to suspect) ridiculing the very idea that anyone should need counseling or medication for any emotional or mental instability. Then, you have a situation in which many kids would rather do anything but acknowledge any need of help.

For parents it's very similar. Just acknowledging that your child has a problem that you cannot fix requires first that you overcome your fears associated with that admission. Then too, you must be willing, for the sake of your child, to risk opening yourself and your actions to possible criticism by introducing him or her into the medical system. Presenting your depressed or anxious child to a doctor or counselor can feel like saying, "Look at me, I'm a terrible parent!" But it's not. And, where your parenting might leave a little to be desired, you are gaining points by making yourself vulnerable in order to enable your child to get the help he or she needs.

If you have recognized that your child needs help, but the child is resistant, keep talking.

Do some research and find what kind of options might be available. Provide a lot of information in order to demystify the process. If you know that other kids in your child's school are getting help, tell your child, *not* who is getting help — protect that child's anonymity — but that you *know for a fact* that your child will not be the only one. If he raises concerns about meeting an acquaintance in a waiting room, tell him how to handle it. Acknowledge your acquaintance cordially; he is not going to mention to the kids at school that he saw you in the counselor or psychiatrist's office. If you yourself have sought counseling in the past, tell your child — not every detail — just that you sought *and found* real help and that it was such a relief just to be able to talk to someone.

One thing that I am glad I did when my kids were adolescents and teens was to talk to them, more than once when it seemed appropriate, about the "dark place." I haven't asked them whether they remember the conversations, but I hope that somehow the words made their way into the recesses of their minds. People go through hard times, I told them, problems, losses and disappointments. We all do! But, especially for a teen or young adult under such circumstances, it can feel for a time as though the problems are insurmountable and absolutely unbearable. It can *feel* as though it could never get better, as though you will never be happy again, but it's not true! It might take some time, but it *will* get better. And you might not be able to handle it alone, but there is real help. You just have to find it and avail yourself of it. And, most importantly, I told them what I myself have learned from experience and which I remember as an encouragement in hard times. Of the "dark place" I tell them, *"It's not a place we go to stay. No, it's just a place we have to walk through."*

It is very important that both we and our children recognize a few truths:

1) Everyone has problems, if not now, then at some time in the future.

2) Kids — and adults — go to counselors, even take medications, and don't advertise the facts. It is almost certain that your child has classmates who are getting help.

3) Isolation in the midst of the crowd is a common experience in our culture, and a counselor serves, first and foremost, as an objective person to hear our hurts and help us to heal.

4) When we are not moving forward away from depression and anxiety, we are moving backward into deeper depression and anxiety. It is very important, especially for kids, to be moving *forward*.

5) Submitting ourselves to a good counselor makes us better people, and providing such counseling to our kids, when they need it, makes us better parents.

Don't be paralyzed by fear, guilt, pride, preoccupation, or busy-ness. Get the help that your child needs. Allow time for the selected therapeutic approach to work. Re-evaluate and adjust your strategy as needed. But, whatever you do, don't just let it slide!

Chapter 10

Circle Up!

It is both frustrating and frightening to see all of the problems faced by American kids today. The sum of them, the complexity, the profundity, and the logistical difficulties inherent in solving them can be absolutely overwhelming. But there can be no dragging of the feet, no shrugging of the shoulders, and no throwing up of the hands. For those who have children in their lives, who work with children, and, even for some of us who maybe haven't yet been so very involved with children, it's time to move.

I was listening to the radio several days ago after I had already planned and begun writing this book, after I had decided in my own heart and mind that, for any generation and under any circumstances, our children's anchoring was far more important than trying to drive the storms away from them. It's a program that I listen to frequently. The host, Hallerin Hill, who has two grown children of his own, often speaks about the importance of family. He speaks often, in fact, of the importance of his own native family. His family, his parents and grandparents before him, served as stable anchors for their children. They didn't have much and they weren't perfect, but they were faithfully present and engaged, and they did all they could to ensure that their kids were anchored. He talks often about the absence of that steady, fortifying dose of family for today's kids.

On this particular day our nation was processing a recent church shooting by a dishonorably discharged, domestic abuser and ex-Air Force man in Sutherland Springs, Texas, that killed 25 and injured 20. Hill's topic was *Saving the Nation.* "We make people in families, not governments," he said, "For those of you who are raising families, it's time to circle the wagons!"

Circle the wagons. That's what we need to do! And yet each one of us as an individual can be a part of that circle. We can be "family," or at least anchor to someone, to a young person. Hill called on grandparents to "take back their kids," to reinstitute Sunday afternoon dinner. He encouraged families to get back into their faith communities. Then he said something very simple and yet profound:

> "Put something there (into "your" kids) that is better than whatever else is being offered. Terrorism is either ideology or desperation and lack of belonging. An empty, dark mind is an incubator for all sorts of (toxic) things. Circle up. Pour into. Start with relationship."

His point is correct. The void of deep relationships, especially deep, caring, mentoring relationships, is clearly taking its toll on our kids. Kids need someone who is willing to invest time, preferably loads of time, pouring into them love, friendship, wisdom, and shared experience, especially real, everyday experience in walking with the true anchor, Jesus Christ.

Because, **"How then will they call on him in whom they have not believed? And how are they to believe in him of whom they have never heard? And**

how are they to hear without someone (showing them)?" — *Romans 10:14* (liberty taken within the parentheses).

Our kids want to see that God is real. As my son said to me at about age 14, "I want to see God work." And they may hear it at church if we take them, but they really need to "see" it in us. This is not to say that they need to see us as saints in white robes always saying "thee" and "thou" and holding our palms together before us or sit with us for hours at a time front of the Bible or any other similarly ridiculous pretension. They need to see us trusting Him in good times and bad, struggling and overcoming, seeking His forgiveness, His will, and His wisdom. They need to see that He can be trusted for both salvation and for life.

In order for us, for our beloved Selfie Generation, for *anyone* to be all that they are meant to be in this life, we must ultimately have our identity and purpose in Christ. If the anchor adult(s) are grounded in Him, it is likely that the child, too, will set anchor and weather the storms largely intact. But our anchors need to be set in order that our kids may be led to embrace the faith. We ourselves can't be found just "riding the tide" or dog paddling to keep our heads above water (spiritually speaking). We must walk the talk and talk the walk, day in and day out. To talk it and not walk it, particularly, will repulse our kids, who know us so well and can see right through us. We have to be real.

And what of the many kids who are floating free, buffeted by the winds and waves on all sides? Neither Mom nor Dad, neither Grandma nor Grandpa, nor older sibling is able; there is no one "at home" to stand in the gap. Where are their anchors? We need to circle up. We need many more volunteer programs, especially in impoverished neighborhoods; more after school and summer activities; more mentors to spend time with kids, to provide a safe place for growth and learning; and even more "sandwich moms" to stuff backpacks with food, if the kids don't have anything to eat. Better somebody than nobody; better a little investment, whatever you can give, than none.

You could be a difference maker, even *the* difference maker for a child. Each one of us — parent or not — can have a place as anchor in the life of a child or teen. Just by being a friend and sharing, in whatever way we can, our experience of a mighty, merciful, and faithful God, we can introduce them to something — to someOne — they can take hold of as did Peter in the waves, someOne who will secure them in the midst of the storms of life that they can one day be, truly and forever, ***anchored.***

One Last Thing... If you enjoyed this book, you can help me tremendously by leaving a review on Amazon. You have no idea how much this would help.

I also want to give you a *one-in-two-hundred chance* to win a **$200.00 Amazon Gift card** as a thank-you for reading this book.

All I ask is that you give me some feedback, so I can improve this or my next book :)

Your opinion is super valuable to me. It will only take a minute of your time to let me know what you like and what you didn't like about this book. The hardest part is deciding how to spend the two hundred dollars! Just follow this link.

http://booksfor.review/selfie

Thanks to all who shared their thoughts and insights for the creation of this book:

TL Holt, *licensed counselor*

Susan Horn, *school board member, church women's director and former children's director*

Pamela Kilburn, *school counselor*

Nancy Moore, *school counselor*

Pamela Neu, *school counselor/ chapel supervisor*

Seth Houser, *camp director/ school recreation director*

Michael Blake, *inpatient pediatrician*

Chris and Erika Pifer, *church youth directors*

Angie Herdman, *church youth worker*

M.C. Blake, *recent college graduate*

Jared Blake, *current college student*

Rebecca Blake, *current college student and many wonderful unnamed teachers, moms, and students over the years*

Source List:

http://prp.jasonfoundation.com/facts/youth-suicide-statistics/, the Jason Foundation, 2017

https://www.teenhelp.com/teen-depression/teen-depression-statistics/, TeenHelp.com, 2016

http://wate.com/2016/05/05/tennessee-teen-suicide-rates-on-the-rise/, Bridgette Bjorio, May 2016

http://time.com/magazine/us/4547305/november-7th-2016-vol-188-no-19-u-s/, Susanna Schrobsdorff, 10/2016

https://www.cdc.gov/healthcommunication/toolstemplates/entertainmented/tips/Suicide Youth.html, CDC,

https://teens.webmd.com/preventing-teen-suicide#1-2, Stephanie S. Gardner, MD, Jan. 2017

https://www.hsph.harvard.edu/news/magazine/guns-and-suicide/, Karin Kiewra, 2008

https://www.amren.com/news/2015/02/report-just-17-black-teens-live-with-parents-54-for-whites-both-low-marks/, Paul Bedard, Feb. 2015

https://www.familyeducation.com/fun/mobile-apps/safety-beyond-facebook-12-social-media-apps-every-parent-should-know-about, Paul Bedard, Washington Examiner, Feb. 12, 2015

https://www.deseretnews.com/article/865669275/The-Lone-Peak-story-What-you-didnt-know-about-affluence-and-teen-suicide.html, Jesse Hyde, Dec. 14, 2016 https://www.theatlantic.com/education/archive/2014/06/most-kids-believe-that-achievement-trumps-empathy/373378/ Jessica Lahey, Jun. 25, 2014

https://www.thespruce.com/cohabitation-facts-and-statistics-2302236, Sheri Stritof, April 13, 2017

Author Bio

Mary Blake was an engineer/computer programmer before she transitioned into the role of road mom, retiring only last May. In a nod to her lifelong propensity for writing, she hung out her writer's shingle less than a year ago. Mary lives in Knoxville, Tenn., with her steadfast husband, three commuting kids, a large overgrown puppy dog, and two idiosyncratic cats. She draws great joy and strength from her faith, family, and friends; from learning; from the created world; from photography; and from writing for a wide variety of applications.

www.ingramcontent.com/pod-product-compliance
Lightning Source LLC
Chambersburg PA
CBHW031405250726

48656CB00002B/551